THE WORLD OF DEW

THE
WORLD OF DEW

Aspects of Living Japan

by

D. J. ENRIGHT

With photographs by Francis Haar

London : SECKER & WARBURG : 1955

TO THE UNION OF GOODWILL
WITH COMMONSENSE

Kangen wa gujin wo yorokobasu
Fair words please fools

Printed in Great Britain by Butler & Tanner Ltd., Frome and London

CONTENTS

ILLUSTRATIONS

(*All photographs by Francis Haar*)

7

FOREWORD

IT is customary in a book of this nature for the author to state his qualifications at the outset—or, as in this case, his lack of them. It is true that I have spent some eighteen months, as a more or less private person, in Japan; and my eyesight is up to normal standards. But my proficiency in the Japanese language is roughly of the kind which, in less genteel countries of the east, used to be known as 'kitchen'. It has been pointed out to me—though not by Japanese, who allow me the exercise of those 'intuitive processes' which in this very book I have held up to a most ungrateful suspicion— that only those who are reasonably expert in the language should presume to write about the people. The answer to this objection is that nobody with the necessary qualifications seems at all ready to undertake the job which I had in mind. The Japanese language is such that by the time you know it sufficiently well for your knowledge to make any vital difference, it is probable that you will be too enervated—if indeed you are nothing worse than enervated—to write about the Japanese people. You may not even notice them any more.

In short, I am unrepentant. We have heard too much about the 'enigmatic East', and the enigma which cannot be re-solved in intelligible human terms had better be eradicated. I have noticed in certain Japanese a rather smug conviction that they and their country are so peculiarly unique and so unfathomably deep that no foreigner can hope to write suc-cessfully about them. This conviction is part of that Japanese self-consciousness which tows in its wake a certain amount of intellectual obscurantism and, worse, a number of possi-bilities for social injustice of one kind and another—a phe-nomenon which this present book, unlike the scholarly angels, rushes in to attack. I use the word 'attack' advisedly. I am not an anthropologist or a sociologist or any other kind of scientist. It will soon be clear to the reader that I am even grinding an axe—fit menial labour for one who so completely lacks scholarship.

This little book does not pretend to reveal the 'truth' about Japan. It may serve to correct certain misconceptions: and I leave it to later books to correct the misconceptions it creates, and to create their own. The truth is only the truth if it is the whole truth, and the whole truth is something which no book can encompass. *Faute de mieux*, I have merely tried to write honestly, because honesty is one of those lesser virtues which an author ought to be able to achieve, and which, when the 'truth' is so utterly beyond us mere humans that we must leave it to scientists and politicians and investigating committees, we ought to respect more than a little.

I had not wanted to write this book. My ambition was to belong to that small and select band of people who have lived in Japan without writing a book about it. The first pressure, I may say, came from the Japanese side. And eventually there sprang up a sort of 'cold war' between the non-existent book and myself, until I had to write the book to save myself from the ghost of it. The only excuse I can offer for its confusion of form is that the scene I have been trying to convey is even more confused. This, alas, is what much of our enigma amounts to—confusion. The country today is so emphatically not what the Japanese in the past have striven to be—a work of art—that to have created a work of art out of describing it would have involved an amount of distortion which even my meagre conscience would not have condoned.

A complete list of acknowledgments would involve too many names; and the owners of some of them it might involve in embarrassment. But I must express my gratitude to the trustees of Kōnan University for offering me a professorship (and it must be admitted that a post in a private institution, exempt as it is from official pressures on either side, has afforded me a degree of liberty which I have no doubt abused), and to their Honourable Mr. Middleman, Professor Edmund Blunden.

My greatest personal debt is to Dr. Bunshō Jugaku, Dean of the Faculty of Arts of Kōnan University, for kindness and assistance in innumerable ways. I fear that his friendship has occasionally led him along paths which he would have preferred to eschew. The fine photographs which illustrate this book were supplied by Mr. Francis Haar at very short notice. Dr. Donald Keene, at present in Kyoto, and Mr. R. H. Blyth, of Tokyo, have been generous in allowing me to make use of their work on Japanese literature. I must also record my thanks to Mr. R. Courtney Browne, host of the King's Arms Hotel in Kobe ('the only English-style tavern in the far east') for details relating to the financial organization of Japanese bars; and to Mr. J. R. Greenwood for suggesting several of the linguistic innovations mentioned at the end of chapter six. And I am grateful to the British Council in Tokyo for making it possible for me to visit a number of Japanese universities of various kinds.

My thanks are due to the authors and publishers of the following books for permission to quote from them:

The Western World and Japan, by G. B. Sansom (The Cresset Press, London).

The Japanese Nation: A Social Survey, by John F. Embree (Rinehart & Co. Inc., New York).

Suye Mura: A Japanese Village, by John F. Embree, (University of Chicago Press).

Japanese Literature, by Donald Keene (John Murray Ltd., London).

The Phoenix Cup, by John Morris (The Cresset Press, London).

Kakemono, by Honor Tracy (Methuen & Co. Ltd., London).

Senryū : Japanese Satirical Verses, Translated and Explained by R. H. Blyth (The Hokuseido Press, Tokyo).
Echoes from a Mountain School, edited by Seikyō Muchaku (Kenkyusha Ltd., Tokyo).

Acknowledgments are also due to the editors of *Encounter* (London), *The Twentieth Century* (London), and *Bungaku-kai* and *The Mainichi* (Tokyo), for permission to use in a different form material which first appeared in their pages. Several of the poems are reprinted from *Encounter, The Listener* and *The New Statesman & Nation.*

Finally, the author's customary and inevitable debt to his wife's patience cries out all the more loudly for acknowledgment in that the subject of this book is still predominantly as they say, 'a man's country'.

Motoyama, Kobe.   *December* 1954.

1 : GODS AND WORKS OF ART*

THE seventeenth-century shogun, Ieyasu, whom Lafcadio Hearn described as the 'wisest of Japanese rulers', authorized the samurai to kill on the spot any person of the three inferior classes guilty of rudeness. 'A samurai is not to be interfered with in cutting down a fellow who has behaved to him in a manner other than is expected.' Ieyasu was not issuing an ordinance likely to throw the inferior classes into terror or to incite the samurai to wholesale massacre. For the expected manner of behaving was firmly established by precept and example and known to all, and the unexpected was defined by default. An anonymous commentator writes thus in a compilation published in London in 1841 : [1] 'Law and established custom, unvarying, known to all and pressing on all alike are the despots of Japan. Scarcely an action of life is exempt from their rigid, inflexible and irksome control ; but he who complies with their dictates has no arbitrary power, no capricious tyranny to apprehend.' They knew exactly what they had to fear ; they could not say that they did not mean to be rude.

Unhappily, as the years passed, and more particularly when Japan was opened to the unpredictable influences of the mysterious west, the criterion of 'the expected' became increasingly inadequate. Situations of an altogether unexpected nature arose. Sometimes the west complained that the rigid principles of Japan were wrong-headed and silly ; sometimes the west exploited those principles. Yet the Japanese felt that they had nothing else to go on, for they were altogether unpractised in the arts of improvisation. And it seems as if, in a nervous terror, they came to choose one fundamental

[1] *Manners and Customs of the Japanese*, quoted by G. B. Sansom in *The Western World and Japan*, London, 1950.

13

law to which every situation should be referred : a law
which told them that they must strive to deny their own
humanity.   This doctrine of original sin was one that had
no realized religion behind it, for the religion of the State
seems altogether inadequate to that monstrous assumption ;
it was born out of a fear of the unknown.   To describe
the Japanese as an eminently puritanical race might amuse
those who are acquainted with the night-life of the country.
But the night-life is completely separate from the life of the
day ;   the city becomes a different thing after dark.   The
old Adam is catered for on a generous scale, but you do not
recognize him when you meet him on the street the next
morning.   The theory is that the natural sinfulness of man
is something which can be disposed of by opening the sluice
gates at prescribed times and in special places.   At other times
and in other places the stream of life will then run clear and
pure and in an expected manner.

It really appears that the Japanese have always had some
kind of grudge against the ' merely human '.   For the sake
of its very existence every race has built up a more or less
complicated system of behaviour ;   however fanciful that
system, at the heart of it is a piece of sound common sense—
the recognition that we are all human.   The Japanese may
be unique in that their unusually complicated system of
behaviour is based not on a recognition of humanity but on
a proud and yet pathetic denial of it.   It may strike the outsider
that they adopted precisely those ideals which by nature they
were least fitted to fulfil.   Unless the race has changed
physically since feudal times, and changed for the worse,
the ideal of the samurai seems a peculiarly inappropriate one
to set up.   How could a country continually visited by
natural disasters on a huge scale—typhoons, floods, land-
slides and earthquakes—ever conceive itself to be the land of
the gods ?   Rather a land accursed by the gods.   Why
should such a country set out to be master of the east when
it cannot catch up on the damage caused by one typhoon
or one rainy season before the next is upon it ?

The intolerably high standards which the Japanese have set for themselves are surely intimately connected with the thread of sudden and desperate violence which runs through their history. Unable to forgive others, they have resorted to assassination ; unable to forgive themselves, they have turned to suicide, in its most agonizing forms. Dr. Inazō Nitobe in his book on Bushido remarks, apropos of the central samurai virtue of self-control, that ' " He shows no sign of joy or anger ", was a phrase used in describing a great character.' To show no sign of joy or anger is to be either a god or a beast ; and as few of us can persist in godhead for very long it is probably unwise to insist on facing ourselves with this exclusive choice. Perhaps the sadness of the average modern Japanese intellectual is that of a continuously disappointed idealist.

In the days of the feudal lords, the individual's loyalty was to his *daimyō*. When the daimyates were broken up under the impact of the west and, in 1871, a central government established, the local loyalties were merged into a national loyalty. Patriotism replaced feudal allegiance. The principle of submission and sacrifice was the same the individual human soul did not gain anything. Moreover the Imperial system had its protective counterpart firmly set in the domestic circle : and the family unit has preserved a degree of feudalism up to today. Hearn, whose admiration for Japanese ways was of course unquestionable, writes thus of marriage in relation to the domestic ancestor cult : ' Affection might and ought to spring up from the relation. But any affection powerful enough to endanger the cohesion of the family would be condemned. A wife might therefore be divorced because her husband had become too much attached to her ; an adopted husband might be divorced because of his power to exercise, through affection, too great an influence upon the daughter of the house.' [1] In the same book Hearn comments that the Japanese race, ' by nature joyous and kindly ', has shown an aptitude for finding ways of ' modifying the harsher

[1] *Japan : An Interpretation*, 1904.

exactions of law and custom '. It is true that relaxation is allowed in, through an artfully contrived back door ; but anyone less incorrigibly romantic than Hearn would have to admit that the race has shown an even greater aptitude for evolving the constrictive laws and customs in the first place. The geisha was a pleasant relaxation of the bonds of a family-arranged marriage—but if the man should mistakenly fall in love with the geisha, then the price of his relaxation was likely to be a double love-suicide. The ' modifications ' of law and custom were as clearly defined, as lawful and customary, as the laws and customs themselves : they were equally ' expected ', and cleverly calculated never to catch up. In the end the first of *The Hundred Articles* (or, *The Legacy of Ieyasu*) prevailed : ' Avoid things that you like and turn your attention to unpleasant duties.'

The surface smoothness with which this process of altern-ate tightening and loosening has worked must always fascinate the foreign observer—up to the point at which he remembers that they are creatures of flesh and blood whom he is observ-ing and not the actors of a sophisticated play. But western admiration of Japan has generally been of a perverse and dangerous kind. We have praised them for being efficient machines (' the only industrious race of the east ') or else for being little works of art (the samurai and the geisha). Certainly we have never done very much by way of encourag-ing them to be content with their humanity—we have only encouraged them in their own errors. In 1904, the year in which this book of Hearn's was published, the war against Russia broke out. Japan won the admiration of the west by the courage of her soldiers and the incredible swiftness of her victory. A period of *japonaiserie* was inaugurated. It became the fashion for devotees to revel in traditions and customs situated at a notably safe distance. Even such incidents as the following, and they were not uncommon, were held up for praise, though not for emulation. A young officer was ordered to leave for the front ; he was a widower and had no relatives to whom his little daughter could be entrusted. So that anxiety over his child might not distract him from his duty, so that he might devote himself single-mindedly to his Emperor, the officer stabbed her to death. One only hopes that he managed to die himself, for his Emperor. Very probably he did.

Japanese art has had many beauties of strict stylization to offer. But it has surely been the artiest of all arts ; its connection with nature has been of the most fragmentary and suggestive kind, its connection with human life tenuous in the extreme. Ezra Pound remarks that Nō is ' a theatre of which both Mr. Yeats and Mr. Craig may approve '—but I doubt whether Yeats, for all his desire to get away from Ibsenite realism on the stage, could ever have achieved any-thing so utterly remote, so independent of life, as is the total impression of Nō. Hokusai, an artisan rather than an artist in the aristocratic sense of that word, is the great exception ; yet even the human subjects of the popular colour prints are chiefly actors—often actors acting geisha parts, that is to say, actors acting actresses. And Utamaro, a master of disem-bodied line, drew women's faces washed clean of emotion— yet he is, I suppose, Japan's nearest approach to a Toulouse-Lautrec. In no western literature of any period has the gap between art and ordinary life been so wide as in the case of Japanese poetry ; and I wonder whether it is fanciful to suggest that this fact accounts for the peculiar seedy squalor of the cities in which a race famous for its aesthetic refinement lives today.

Utamaro's women are beautiful in their peripheral way. And the traditional virtues of discipline, obedience, loyalty and fortitude have produced their beauties in life ; acts of courage, devotion and self-sacrifice, and a kind of domestic orderliness which persisted through lengthy periods of civil disorder. A Japanese would be careful not to inflict his personal sorrows on anyone else, where a member of any other race would be only too ready to do so. As John F. Embree says, ' If an honourable guest calls on one when one's wife is seriously ill in a back room, one must not trouble the guest by mentioning the fact but on the contrary must make the guest happy with light talk and a treat of wine.' [1] In a similar spirit, perhaps, a maid whom we once employed interspersed with huge bursts of laughter her lurid account of how some child had been reduced to minced meat on the local railway line. A Japanese would be equally careful not to inflict *on*, a feeling of obligation, on anyone else, since sooner or later it would have to be paid off. Bernard Leach, one of those few foreigners whose work in Japan has been wholly and unconditionally for the good of all concerned, told me how one night in Tokyo he bumped into one of those many redundant poles and posts with which Japanese streets are beset. He was dazed by the fall and he had lost his spectacles, but passers-by studiously avoided him, until at last an American soldier came to the rescue. I doubt whether he would have been much consoled by the account which Miss Ruth Benedict gives in *The Chrysanthemum and the Sword* of the thought-patterns surrounding the concept of *on*. (There is of course the possibility that the passers-by may, very mistakenly, have supposed the prostrate figure to be that of a drunken foreigner whom it would be wise to avoid : so much modern behaviour, native and foreign, sends one yearningly back to the well-ordered past.[2]) The acts of virtue in which Japanese social

[1] *The Japanese Nation : A Social Survey*, 1945.

[2] A Japanese friend comments that what deterred passers-by from aiding Mr. Leach was their ignorance of English : they would not be able to ask the foreign gentleman what he was searching for. That is true, up to a point, for Japanese are generally very ready to help foreigners. It still seems a pity that the fear of embarrassment should stand in the way of charity. And this explanation obviously does not cover the case of a respectably dressed blind Japanese who is left to blunder hopelessly among stacks of bicycles along a busy pavement. No, there is a good deal of callousness in ' public behaviour ' in present-day Japan. But then, the individual who ' weakens ' will be lost : so many lame dogs, so many stiles. Japan is the testing-ground of humanism. An excess of man and an insufficiency of man's means : if your faith in man survives this test, it is impregnable.

history is rich have always been for the sake ultimately of something greater than humanity—something which, when one tries to locate it, doesn't seem to be convincingly there.

' Let us not be mere humans—we must be gods, or, at second best, works of conscious art.' This animus against the human, this urge to be the one race that should successfully avoid the implications of common humanity, was increased by Japan's early contacts with the outside world. No doubt the foreigners with whom they had to deal were not always of the best kind, but it was certainly a manifestation of the mythopoeic streak in the national character that held all foreigners to be foul-smelling and hairy barbarians devoid of toes.[1] Japanese agoraphobia grew rapidly. Whenever they found something to admire in foreign customs (say, a superior kindliness towards animals), then immediately afterwards they found something to erase that admiration (perhaps the public execution of criminals). At all events they must dissociate themselves from these all-too-human foreigners. And so the race became increasingly self-conscious about its divine origin—helped on of course by assiduous politicians and other interested bodies—until the grand climax came with the astounding attack on Pearl Harbour. And then the *dénouement* followed, slowly at first. And then, an equally astounding anti-climax, the atom bombs on Hiroshima and Nagasaki.

Where were the Japanese then? Perhaps still, though now more ruefully, totting up the foreigners' accounts. The foreigners treated their prisoners of war far better—and yet they dropped atom bombs on the civilian population of a country already defeated. . . . All-too-human, all-too-human.

But the rest of the story is happier—or, at least, it holds out the promise of happiness. The atom bombs had one good result : they made the myth of the samurai, strutting about with his two feeble swords, look remarkably silly. Indeed, the catastrophe was in one way a shocking caricature and a

[1] Just as even today the legend still persists that the *eta*, the pariahs of Japan, are born without thumbs.

ghastly showing up of the samurai myth : in the past a
samurai might go out at night to test a new sword on the
first passer-by, and here were the western powers testing their
new weapon on the Japanese people.   The ensuing military
occupation surely did more good than harm.   If Allied policy
was confused, contradictory and sometimes plain ignorant,
then the Japanese too were confused, contradictory and
sometimes plain ignorant.   It is easy to make merry—in the
manner of Miss Honor Tracy's book *Kakemono*—over the
farcical goings-on of the American saviours in Japan at this
period, yet in a sense the naïvety of their conception of
democracy accorded well with the naïvety of the Japanese
people in defeat.   Miss Tracy's sophistication has something
in common with the sophistries of the old Japanese militarists,
after all.   The Japanese took their defeat and the occupation
with a remarkable lack of resentment, and the occupation
itself was humane ; neither side was able to summon up
sufficient moral indignation for it to be otherwise, both sides
were chastened.   The use of the atom bomb had robbed the
allies of whatever moral advantage they might have derived
from the barbarity with which their enemies had conducted
the war ; and the effects of the bomb forced the Japanese to
realize that they were in no practical sense the children of the
gods but simply flesh and blood and all-too-mortal.

In *The Phoenix Cup* John Morris touches on one of the
most pathetic aspects of this realization of humanity.   Japanese soldiers expected to die when they were captured.   Though
they were not killed by their captors, most of them considered
themselves dead, dead to their country and their families.
' Once I was an out-and-out militarist, and I became a p.o.w.
Now that I am dead I have told you my whole story.' [1]
Eventually they were returned to their homes, often unwill-
ingly, to find that in some cases they were in fact officially dead.
Their relatives received them first of all with shame—and
then, for the greater part, with love.   The cities were in ruins,

[1] *The Phoenix Cup* (' Some Notes on Japan in 1946 '), by John
Morris, London, 1947.

people were starving to death in the streets, the whole social edifice had crashed—there was no other course possible than that victors and vanquished should work together in an atmosphere which sheer emergency had rendered free from moral recriminations and self-conscious attitudes.

But a national crisis slowly changed into the daily hardships and discomforts of life in an impoverished and disorganized country. Moreover, Japan's emergency dissolved into a series of world emergencies. The new and largely welcome ideas of democracy, liberty of choice and personal responsibility were found to be capable of diverse interpretations—an inconvenience which had not attached to the rigid traditional conceptions. The great war which Japan had recently fought began to seem as nothing compared with what was on the way—merely a minor clash from which no really and permanently useful lesson could be learnt after all, which proved nothing and disproved nothing.

All my sympathies are with the young Japanese of today, whether a young writer, the young man in the street or the young woman who manages to keep off the streets. They have had a raw deal from history—from both their own ancient history and contemporary world history too. The rest of the world has praised their country for the wrong things and failed to praise them for the right; it has condemned them for their violence without proposing any remedy for the disease which lies at the heart of that violence. In a number of ways, indeed, the rest of the world has encouraged that violence, sometimes romantically and sometimes cynically. The young Japanese is bewildered and unsure—how could he be otherwise?—but he is chastened and only too eager to be sensible, to find some way of living and letting live. And now the world will not let him. We point him back to those chains which he has started to throw off—traditions of insular culture, the valour and self-sacrifice of the warrior ideal, the convenient ability to exist in apparent peace at a little above starvation level. It is bitter to read what Mr. Morris wrote only eight years ago concerning the two main tasks of the Army of Occupation : ' First of all there is what might be described as the immediate military problem of destroying Japan's *capacity*, both actual and potential, again to be a menace to the peace of the world.   The second, which is a long-term objective, is the destruction of Japan's *will* to be aggressive.' The first aim was accomplished very easily, and now, less easily, it is being undone, since there is no such thing as ' the peace of the world ' to be menaced and Japan has acquired an impressive new status as the main bulwark against Communism in the east.   The second aim, as Mr. Morris said, was a long-term policy ; even though it has been granted no long term, it has succeeded to an extent which Japan's guardians and sponsors now find embarrassing.

The mirror of Yamato is indeed clouded.   How can the student help but be confused by the scurrying contradictions which beset him when his teachers themselves are torn between *schadenfreude* and dismay ? A lecturer of Tokyo (ex-Imperial) University writes thus in the newspaper : ' American occupation of Japan and demobilization of Japanese armed forces proceeded smoothly.   The Japanese people entertained a great joy over the fact that the source of their misery, the military forces, had been eliminated. . . . To what extent (i.e. *nine years after the end of the war*) have the Japanese become democratic ?   Look at the situation in agrarian communities and a ready answer will be available.   They are gradually " correcting " the excessive occupation policies. Under a patriarchal authority, people are beginning to observe the traditional patterns. . . .   It is an overt fact that it is the rural communities that are the " home ground " of the most pro-American Liberal Party and that it is these rural communities where American policy of democratization suffered the severest defeat. . . .   Is it a matter of coincidence of history or due to the absence of principles and policy in politics that the failure of Occupation policies in Japan is now acclaimed as a success and the success condemned as a failure ? '

To escape from one's national history only to be entrapped in world history is a tragic irony.   This book—if I could have succeeded—would have been an account of that tragedy in human terms—the terms which the Japanese are painfully learning just at the moment when the great powers of the world are preparing to forget them.

Every book on Japan written since 1870 has stated the theme of ' Japan in Transition '. The author of a book published in 1910 prophesied confidently that in ten years the Boys' Festival would have vanished, yet in 1954 from the fifth of May onwards huge cloth carps, the symbol of manly stoicism and perseverance, were flying from every house which contained a son. Perhaps I am falling into the same error of conceit—for every writer tends to feel that he has created the important thing he is describing—yet I think that only now is Japan far enough into its transitional stage to be truly described as ' *in* transition '. Unfortunately the commentator can no longer deal with Japan as a self-contained and neatly bundled entity, for she is open on all sides to the rest of the world, and the world is ' in transition '.

2 : THE LITTLE KNOWLEDGE

'Here! is this you on the top of Fan-kuo Mountain,
Wearing a huge hat in the noon-day sun?
How thin, how wretchedly thin, you have grown!
You must have been suffering from poetry again.'
                    (*Li Po, trans. Shigeyoshi Obata*)

'When I look back to my past days I find myself
envying the precarious position of high officials, or
sometimes thinking of becoming a Buddhist monk.   But
after all I have come to make my livelihood by resigning
myself to floating clouds and wind and flowers and birds.
In choosing this way of life, Li Po has ruptured himself,
and old Tu Fu has grown wretchedly thin, just like me,
though I am without any genius.'
                    (*The Japanese poet, Bashō*)

LET us begin, as so many Japanese discussions begin, with a
word. *Sensei.* A magic word, and yet very equivocal.
Sensei means 'teacher' plus 'scholar' plus 'beloved master';
it means intellect, learning, culture, taste; it means China,
tanka, haiku, Nō plays, pottery, Zen.   It means head in the
clouds, hermit, thinker.   Yet it also means 'those who can't
do, teach', a reciter of old lecture notes, the over-worked
and under-paid servant of a government institution or a
private corporation, a man who hasn't the wit to grow rich
by shifting theoretical money from one bank to another, the
uneasy tenant of an Ivory Tower that an atom bomb has
fallen on.   It means one who lives and moves in 'another
world' and had better stay there; it means one who is
supposed to be willing to starve in order to write a commentary on a commentary; and it also means someone who must
turn out popular journalism or give private lessons in 'Com-

mercial English' in order to buy the food which would enable him to write a commentary on a commentary if only he had the time. In fact, to those who manage this world, the word signifies something not unlike the bar hostess—a little recreation which one can well afford, more respectable of course and more highbrow, but still the tired business man's entertainment, something which is essentially peripheral. There is a *senryū*, a short satirical poem, which hints at this aspect of the word *sensei*:

> Sensei to
> iwareru hodo no
> baka de nashi.[1]

'We Japanese respect the *sensei*,' says the nimble business man. Yes, but you know that he is worth no more than the salary he gets.[2] And now that the other-worldliness of the *sensei*—something at which both academics and the rest of society have connived—is breaking down, there is the fear that when he speaks out, the *sensei* may speak in the language of Marx. This reaction from isolation to demagogy is only one example among many of the violence with which Japan escapes from its traditions.

In my own experience, Japanese academics are gentle, sincere in their scholarship and, outwardly at any rate, surpassingly modest. As persons they compare well with the run of English academics: the latter are prone to regard their proficiency in some out-of-the-way subject as a sign of moral superiority. Like their colleagues in other countries,

---

[1] 'I am not such a fool as to be called *sensei*.'

[2] A first-grade professor in a first-grade university (comparable to the occupant of a chair in a British university) will earn about £40 per month. The salary of 'senior lecturers' is roughly £30, and that of 'junior lecturers'—who may be well over 30 years of age since academic seniority comes distressingly late here—roughly £20 per month. These salaries are net, but even so incomes have to be made up in a variety of ways, some of them not too arduous, none of them conducive to scholarship or peace of mind.

Japanese academics are inclined to specialize in subjects which would seem no concern of anyone with any respect for his own humanity; unworthy specialization is aggravated by academic over-population, which is probably worse in Japan than anywhere else. But they are not intellectual snobs. They drive themselves hard, but they live at peace with their colleagues.

The favourite fairy story of the two old men, Yoi Ojiisan who was merry and good and Warui Ojiisan who was miserable and bad, seems to have been turned upside-down where *sensei* are concerned. For melancholy—or something apparently more extreme—appears to be considered a sure sign of superior scholarship and of superior morality as well.[1] My wife is acquainted with two heads of departments occupying identical positions in two neighbouring state universities. They are completely dissimilar in personality, for the one is relentlessly gloomy and the other irrepressibly lively. Travelling home in the train one day she mentioned to a student who had struck up a conversation (or perhaps an English Conversation Lesson) with her that she had just heard one of these professors giving a very witty talk. 'Ah, but do you know Professor Y?' enquired the student earnestly,

[1] Cf. Sir George Sansom on the conception of education in feudal Japan: '. . . not less indispensable to a teacher than learning was a high character which should influence the moral development of his pupils; and the reverence in which great teachers were held was called forth not by their skill in expounding nor by their store of knowledge, but by exemplary conduct and lofty principles.' Perhaps it is because the largeness of modern classes precludes this diffusing of morality that, though I have known several Japanese teachers of high moral character and highly esteemed by their pupils, I have not observed their influence to sink very deep—at least not to the extent of persuading the pupils to give up their seats in the trains to old or pregnant women. But perhaps my conception of morality is insular and naïve.

On the whole my sympathies are with the business-like approach to education which Yukichi Fukuzawa, the 'modernist' and founder of Keio University, expounded in the 1870's: 'What is

mentioning the other gentleman's name, 'now *he* is a *good* man'. My wife attempted to worm some kind of definition of this ' goodness ' out of the student, but in the end she was left with the very clear impression that the first professor was looked down upon because he was amusing and successful while the second was looked up to because he was chronically wretched and obviously unsuccessful. A kind of virtue, impalpable but powerful, is set upon gloominess ; it is often associated with profundity in intellectual circles, as the abnormal success which authors such as Kafka, Eliot, Sartre, Greene and their followers have had here might suggest. Those Americans who interpret the current complainings and grim prognostications regarding the hydrogen bomb tests as Communist-inspired anti-Americanism might console themselves that in part at any rate it is an orthodox acknow-ledgment of the futility of human life, it is a form of *aware*, the sad ' ah-ness ' of things. But the sadness of the *sensei* is not harsh or disgruntled ; the Japanese teacher is not of the type who takes out his personal bitterness on his students ; his melancholy is of the gentle variety, perhaps of the variety which in happier days we used to call ' poetic '.

This being so, one would expect relations between students

really wanted is learning that is close to the needs of a man's daily life. A man who can recite the Chronicles but does not know the price of food, a man who has penetrated deeply into the classics and history but cannot carry out a simple business transaction—such people as these are nothing but rice-consuming dictionaries, of no use to their country but only a hindrance to its economy.' The 479 Japanese universities of today might seem a melancholy result of Fukuzawa's drive against the old conception of education as a dignified luxury for the few. Yet he could still ask of what use to the students' lives are most of the subjects they so laboriously study. Of what use will the information about Ezra Pound and T. S. Eliot which my students insist on getting from me be to them when they are sitting on office stools wrestling with some ' simple business transaction ' couched in the language they are supposed to have specialized in ?

and teachers to be more intimate than in England. But this is not the case. Relations remain formal in the extreme. If I ask for a question, most probably I get none; if I ask for an answer, none is forthcoming. Very occasionally, however, some kind-hearted student who wants to make the foreigner feel at home will manage to bring out a question. Yet from his manner, and the general uneasiness of the class, one realizes that, for all his good intentions, there exists a feeling that he is being rude to you. To ask a question implies that the *sensei* has not done his job properly—moreover, he might not know the answer, in which case the questioner is responsible for his loss of face.[1] The atmosphere is much the same if I ask a question of the class—though presumably in that case the rudeness is mine. They freeze, they look intensely as if they were not there at all. I am sure that their feelings are both complicated and good. They do not want to lose face by offering a wrong answer, nor do they wish me to lose face through my responsibility for their wrongness; nor do they wish to seem cleverer than their class-mates. After begging them time and time again to make a guess, finally, faced with their communal solidarity, I bring out the right answer myself in a kind of apoplexy, having lost more face than I ever possessed. Much of the time many of them knew the answer all along—knowing that I must answer it myself, I never ask a difficult question—and would be very happy to go home and write a long essay on it. But to take the floor implies ' competition ', and there is little competitive spirit in Japan : to seem brilliant is to become suspect, and silence is the speech of a wise man.

Indeed it would seem sometimes that silence—as well as melancholy—is identified with intellectual profundity. ' Full vessels make the least noise ' might well be a Japanese proverb : it is as true as the one which says that ' not to know is to be a

---

[1] However irritated by the touchy concern which Japanese evince for their ' face ', the foreigner has to admit that they show an equal concern to preserve immaculate the ' face ' of others.

Buddha '. I recall a conversation with a distinguished Professor (with a capital ' p ') of English in Tokyo ; I was praising the students of a certain women's college for their quick comprehension of spoken English and their comparatively uninhibited speaking of English. The conversation went like this

'. . . I must admit that it makes a pleasant change from men students.'

Professor : ' Ah, but it does not mean very much. They do not understand inside them.'

' They don't feel it, you mean ? ' (So the speechless young men, so busy thinking that there isn't a chance for a word to come out, are to be prized above those articulate—and rather decorative —young ladies ? However, the Professor is a very kind man, in act as well as in silent theory, whose genuineness as a man and as a scholar shines out unmistakably. He has been teaching Japanese students all his life, he must know more about it than I. And so, feeling like a cad . . .) ' You mean that they make good office typists ? '

The Professor roared with amusement. That was exactly what he meant. A week later and my *bon mot* had reached academic circles at the other end of the country. It was a comment in Dr. Nitobe's *Bushido* that brought the conversation back to my mind : ' To give in so many articulate words one's inmost thoughts and feelings—notably the religious— is taken among us as an unmistakable sign that they are neither very profound nor very sincere. " Only a pomegranate is he "—so runs a popular saying—" who, when he gapes his mouth, displays the contents of his heart." ' All the same, I still wonder whether men who cannot understand English are more likely to have profound and creditable reactions to English literature than women who can understand English. If the classes I have taught in Japan ever produce a creative genius, perhaps it will be a male. But if the same classes produce ten people capable of reading foreign literature with understanding, with modesty and without soul-tempests, I imagine that seven of them will be women.

My first supposition was that this painful lack of discussion —painful in that the teacher must do all the work all the time—was due to their weakness in spoken English. But I found that classes conducted by Japanese teachers in Japanese operated in exactly the same fashion ; and I suspect that now I am getting more questions than my Japanese colleagues. The latter tell me, ' Discussion in class is not a Japanese tradition.' The student is told ; he does not ask and he is not asked. Lest any romantic should put this state of affairs down to the evils of an unsuitable post-war ' democracy ', it should be noted that at the very beginning of this century Baron Kikuchi, a Cambridge graduate and erstwhile President of Tokyo Imperial University who became Minister of Education, said, ' We are beset by the evil of excessive cramming . . . In most of our elementary schools the books are galloped through, pupils being required to write down as much as possible of what falls from the teachers' lips.' The exception to the tradition is the deliberately topsy-turvy and madcap teaching of Zen Buddhism. There the relationship between master and novice is consciously un-traditional, since the master is striving not to fill the novice's mind but to empty it or even to get rid of it for the time being ; and the student knows that the last thing he will get to his sensible question is a sensible answer :

A monk asked Unmon, ' What is the Buddha ? ' ' A dry shit-stick,' replied Unmon.[1]

In some subjects presumably it does not matter that the student believes the teacher all the time. But in literature, where the important part depends upon personal judgments, the teacher can hardly contemplate with equanimity his every word passing into his students' note-books with all the authority of Holy Writ. How many times have I had to make the class cross out some ill-considered remark of mine ;

[1] *Haiku* (Vol. I, *Eastern Culture*), by R. H. Blyth, Tokyo, 1949.

how often, as I have passed from one way of putting it to another, have they ended with the most magnificently mixed metaphors in their note-books ! Then what can the student do who thinks otherwise from his teacher ? I asked the question of a Japanese acquaintance, who replied, ' In that case he must leave his master and seek another. But there cannot be any show of open disagreement.' Yet when I mentioned this barrier between student and teacher to a meeting of Japanese university teachers, they told me that the barrier was by no means so impregnable as it had been before the war—indeed, I gathered that they considered it pretty flimsy and were even a little nervous lest it should collapse altogether. And that is comprehensible. When the Japanese abandon a traditional standpoint they tend to swing violently to its contrary extreme ; and from silent respect the student-body might swing to vocal disrespect— students without masters might turn out as dangerous as were the *rōnin* (' wave-men '), the masterless samurai. That such a reaction would be only temporary and that healthier teaching would result from it I do not doubt ; but I can sympathize with the unfortunate *sensei*, who would have to witness a further fall in their stock.

I was about to remark that Japanese academics are the most academic in the world. In spite of this being a rash generalization,[1] there is a certain truth in it. It is distressing in the extreme to see a man wearing out his eyes on collecting footnotes to *Beowulf*, to all intents already blind to the world around him— especially when everything worth saying about that poem has already been said several times, and moreover

[1] There are ' Three Ways of Reading '—' Reading in the Saddle ' (in modern terms, reading in bus or train) ; ' Reading on the Pillow ' (in bed, as we should say) ; and ' Reading in the *Benjo* ' (a comfortless environment, one would have thought : the Japanese lavatory is distinguished as being one of the very few things Japanese which no foreigner has rhapsodized over). A celebrated professor and scholar tells me that a popular weekly has just commissioned him to write an essay on the third Way.

the man cannot speak ordinary modern English. There are many teachers of the younger generation who are interested in modern European literature, yet among both young and old there is this striking preference for language over literature and for the dead over the living. Every university library of any standing, and even some of the junior colleges, have shelves given up to the expensive publications of the Early English Text Society. Whatever else may be missing—and library allocations are not generous at present—you will be sure to find such standard classics as ' The Book of Fayttes of Armes and of Chyualrye', ' Lincoln Diocese Documents', ' The Blickling Homilies of the Tenth Century' and ' Arderne's Treatises of Fistula in Ano (Haemorrhoids and Clysters)'. That there should be more people researching on and teaching language than literature is not surprising, for a just appreciation of English literature depends upon an intimacy with the language which few *sensei* are able to achieve. How can they afford to go to England ? It is sad to think how many never visit the country which they have spent their lives talking and thinking and writing about. Language study, however, requires only the schematizing ability which the Japanese are strong in. I once attempted to give ' advanced ' language lessons to a group of colleagues, but whereas they knew the rules, I only knew what one could say and what one couldn't : it was an unfair battle. My efforts to deal with the ' anomalous finites ' were similarly disastrous as I soon discovered that my audience had been brought up on Professor H. E. Palmer's system, while I was still only trying to understand it. It can hardly be said that the standard of spoken and written English in Japan generally reflects much credit on Palmer's technique—he was Linguistic Adviser to the Japanese Department of Education at one time and Director of the Tokyo Institute for Research in English Teaching—but the Japanese, with their touching loyalty to anyone who has worked in their country, will hear no ill of it.

It seems offensive to be making these criticisms. One forgets that with the sheer mass of English study that goes on here it is only to be expected that a considerable part of it should be in some way invalidated or unsuccessful. To compare English studies in Japan with Japanese studies in England would not be appropriate—but compare them with French and German studies and I think it must be admitted that Japanese academics, with almost nothing but sheer persistence and good will in their favour, have gone further towards conquering an altogether foreign culture than one would have thought possible. What depresses me is the stress placed on philology—there appears to be an obscure feeling that the philologist is a superior person to the literary man, a feeling that literature is a popularization and a debasement of language—and also the way in which literature tends to get divorced from its social context and, as far as possible, purged of its human relevance. Japanese students are great collectors of ' ideas ' : the idea that ideas might be translated into action, or that in poetry they have emotional connotations or concomitants which are equally important, too often escapes them. Told that such and such a work is Christian in tendency or Utilitarian or Liberal, they are contented. That is one type of student : the type who conforms to what we might call the Ivory Tower legend, the legend assiduously fostered by the samurai (who tossed off a tasteful poem as easily as he tossed off an enemy's head) and the politician and the business man.

But then there is the other type : the type who belongs to the violent reaction against the Ivory Tower, the student who takes ' ideas ', divorced from their context of style, so seriously that he almost dies under the strain. If the first assumes that literature has nothing much to do with life, the second is apt to identify literature with life. It is the latter type that is producing the young writer, and he is of course a more sympathetic person than the former, for he is sincere and he is ' committed '. But what is he committed to ? Too often it seems that he is committed less to contemporary Japanese life than to contemporary, or more accurately a little less than contemporary, European literature. *The Waste*

C

Land has been moved from Europe, rather in the fashion of
' The Ghost goes West ', and set down in the Far East.
Admittedly it fits rather neatly—an English friend remarked
that

> What are the roots that clutch, what branches grow
> Out of this stony rubbish ?

might well have been asked of post-war Tokyo. But the
trouble is that the Japanese are inclined to take it all too
literally. *The Waste Land* is an ambivalent work. Regarded as an ' idea ' it is, I believe, highly inaccurate, preju-
diced and dangerous. But as a poem, a poem which brought
life back into poetry, it is paradoxically a demonstration of
human vitality. ' Modern ' though it was, it had its links
with the past, and its style—demonstrating the persistence of
the human spirit—modified the destructive trend of its
thought. A full recognition of English tradition is beyond
the majority of Japanese, especially as their own traditions
tend to be static, to break but not to bend ; and for all their
undoubted sensitiveness it is not likely that they will give
sufficient weight to the invigorating rhythmical processes and
stimulating imagery of the poem. What is left—only too
accessible to them—is the residue of unrelieved pessimism
and disgust. There is no past, there is no future. *The
Waste Land*, having been universally recognized as a great
poem, is therefore final proof that the world is waste : confirmation is conveniently provided by Greene, Sartre, Rilke,
Kafka, Somerset Maugham, Aldous Huxley, Evelyn Waugh,
Jean Genêt, Henry Miller and others.

I feel—though my feelings carry little authority—that the
classical forms of Japanese poetry have come to the end of
their road and that for a society so different from that in which
they arose different forms will be required. If feeling changes
—as I hope and believe it is doing—then form must change
too : yet experiment in poetic form, at any rate up to the
1920's, has been negligible. But this is the subject of a later
chapter, and here I only wish to suggest that though Japanese

poets of today may well find inspiration from the study of contemporary western poets, yet to christen the yearly anthology of anti-traditional Japanese poets with the name of *Wasteland* (' Arechi ') is to damn it from the start.

The Japanese people contrive to be, at times, the saddest people in the world : their relaxed faces in the train look like tragic masks.   At other times, they turn out to be perhaps the happiest people in the world, in their quiet way and at little expense—a father and his children flying kites, the un-rehearsed dancing during the Buddhist festival of *Bon*, the Feast of All Souls, the men who heave the shrine-on-wheels when the god goes out to inspect his parish, the girls chattering under the cherry blossom.   They have few material reasons for being happy at present : the atom bomb was still reverber-ating when the hydrogen bomb threw the fish markets into a panic : and yet they achieve happiness, perhaps to a greater extent than an outsider can guess.   It makes me feel guilty to see piles of translations of Greene, Kafka, Sartre, Dos Passos, Genêt and so forth in the book-shops—and to see the dejected face of the average young Japanese intellectual, who walks as if he had the sorrows of the world on his shoulders and the nitrogen bomb in his brief-case.   (Mind you, forty years have passed since Yone Noguchi remarked, somewhat complacently, ' I should like to know where is a Japanese poet who is not sad.')   I sometimes feel that he will believe anything—as long as it is bad enough.   And that his poems are likely to be as ' academic '—I mean as far removed from the living heart of his own people—as are the enfeebled and puerile whimsies of the average amateur *tanka* poet.   Yet, after so long a period of stagnation in poetry, perhaps the reaction had to be hectic and disordered.   Perhaps the period of stabilization is already setting in.   And who are we, in the west, to complain if it isn't ?   How many of us write without the shadow of *The Waste Land* falling across our pages ?

When I published in *Encounter* an article dealing with the immense—and, as I think, predominantly unhappy—influ-ence of such writers as Joyce, Eliot and Greene in Japan, the

Times Literary Supplement was sufficiently interested to suggest in a leading article that what my students lacked was a sense of the 'background' of English literature.[1] That was certainly one of my points—that the Japanese intellectual (and it was Japanese intellectuals that I had in mind rather than university students) tends to see *The Waste Land* or *Ulysses* or *Les Chemins de la Liberté* or *England Made Me* against only the still present background of Japanese *après-guerre*, and that his rather naïve acceptance of these works tends to persuade him that since the world is wholly and irrevocably waste there is nothing left to do but rake over the broken fragments in the hope of finding an interesting bit of exquisite horribleness. But I had also wished to suggest that part of the fault lay in those works themselves. That *The Waste Land* itself, if examined coolly and without the aid of the orthodox commentaries, yielded evidence that the scales had been tampered with, that the grey had consistently been darkened to black, and that the bitterness of his animus had sometimes tempted the poet into an imagery of disgust which was even childish in its strained over-statement and its generalizing ('the broken fingernails of dirty hands') and a tone of voice tinged with pomposity ('I Tiresias have fore-suffered all . . .'). I do not know whether anyone has suggested that parts of the poem are open to precisely the criticism which Eliot has brought against *Hamlet*: that an adequate 'objective correlative' is lacking. It must be due to the fact that the menacing emotions which hover around the three Thames Daughters at the end of the third section are 'in excess of the facts as they appear', that I am left with the uncomfortable impression of having spent a lot of time in various countries warning young ladies against the perils of boating parties.

However that may be, it was certainly not my intention to

[1] In teaching the *Shoemaker's Holiday* it requires a great effort of mind to recall the fact that Japanese shoemakers are mainly of the *eta* or pariah class. But the fact should add zest to one's teaching.

patronize Japanese intellectuals. We cannot blame them for failing to revalue what we have not revalued ourselves. Perhaps the best comment on the situation was made in an end-of-term report by one of my girl students, by way of accounting for the popularity in this country of Sartre, Camus, Rilke, Eliot and Greene. She wrote, 'Their darkness and sarcasm and negative spirit have attracted much attention in Japan, for it is natural to be welcomed these points in absence of mind after war.'

In stressing the 'melancholy' of Japanese intellectuals, I have been less than just to them as human beings. In general they are—and particularly the younger ones—a gentle, sensitive and sympathetic race. And after all is said perhaps a settled sadness is preferable to the forced gaiety with which European intellectuals attempt to hide their lack of consequence. One meets many writers and artists who are not doing well out of literature or art : they do not repine, for they had never expected to do well, and they have the pleasure of their work. In Japan you will still find the genuinely Bohemian type who is practically extinct in Europe —I do not mean the noisy, arty and 'shocking' kind of individual (indeed such a person would be hard to find in Japan), but quite simply the person whose preoccupation with his work, whether his work is good or bad, is such that he can endure neglect and poverty without noticing it : his illusions do not lie that way, and his remoteness from the world of politics and business has a modesty about it and is free from arrogance or bitterness.

No doubt the established writers of Japan (they seem mainly to be writers of fiction, with a few social and political essayists thrown in) behave in much the same way as our own established writers. But the typical struggling writer or artist bears himself with a dignity which one sees little of among his contemporaries in England : there is none of that cocktail party ethos here, the log-rolling, the wooing of useful contacts and the little favours. Free from material self-seeking, in a spirit of single-minded and even primitive devotion, the Japanese only wants the best of the world of art—the young English writer too often wants the best of both worlds and ends by getting the second-best of each. (Not that any member of the Security State is really in a position to complain on this score : it is a matter which the artist must settle with his own conscience.) I do want to make it clear that this Japanese sadness of which I have spoken should not be confused with the bitterness of the man who is only too aware that he has got the worst of both worlds. It has been a privilege to meet people who take a quiet joy in their work and are not a nervous prey to ' audience ' anxiety and the consciousness of the public eye.[1]

One finds the urge to understand Z before comprehending A in students of all kinds and countries, of course. Here in Japan it is more pronounced, I think, and more obstinate than elsewhere. The effects of the impact of western litera- ture on the youth of the Middle East and the Far East have often brought me near to tears. What can one say ? One's first impulse is to cry, ' Never mind—forget it all—relax ! ' But then one settles down to try to explain whatever the difficulty seems to be—to explain, perhaps, the basic tenets of Christianity, warning them at the same time that this may

[1] A quiet joy—yes, but I am always alarmed by the intensely nervous, even feverish, way in which they work. For example, Japanese magazines have a habit of issuing an invitation and requesting delivery of completed manuscript within two or three days : I had thought this an instance of editorial arrogance, until I learned that writers actually liked it that way. I have met authors who habitually return home after *sake*-drinking at mid- night, sleep for four or five hours, and then start work. The manager (and cook) of the eel-restaurant *Itohei* in Kobe closes down at 11 p.m. or so and goes home to paint. The foreigner who tries to impress Japanese with his own busy-ness will cut no ice at all : the Japanese are always harder-pressed. They enjoy this condition, apparently, but whether they thrive on it is another matter. Urgency is the catalyst in their creative processes : they despise sleep and dispense with its services as far as possible, not always (I fear) to their real advantage.

have nothing to do with literature precisely, that George Herbert is a great poet and Bishop Heber a very little one. And to explain the fundamentals of Christianity seems immensely difficult all of a sudden—even though everyone is too nice to bring up the atom bomb—and for all the world as if one didn't understand it oneself. And so, after an exhibition which would discredit a kindergarten Bible class, one falls back on whatever one can offer in the way of impromptu personal advice : ' Even though you grasp the matter, you can't fully grasp the style—so at this stage don't take literature *too* seriously. Live a bit—and read afterwards. And for God's sake—your god or mine or anybody else's—remember that life is more important than literature and don't let the latter mess up the former. Make a poem out of your life, if you must—but don't make your life out of somebody else's poem, especially if it's *The Waste Land*. . . .'

Here, to end the chapter on a gentler note, is a letter I have just received from a girl student of Kobe University who followed a course of mine on modern English poetry. I quote it in full because the beginning and end—though they have no relevance to our discussion—are delightfully Japanese-lady-like :

What on earth are you getting along in these very hot days ? I'm alright and trying to study hard. But in spite of my determination, I enjoyed short journey often—to Tokyo, Takamatsu, Ise and Toba.

As I before told you, I intend to study of ' T. S. Eliot ' for my graduating subject. But Eliot is so difficult. I wish to understand his fundamental idea, and to do so I have to understand ' What is Catholicism '.

As I am not Christian, moreover I have few knowledge about Christianity, it is not quite simple for me to get much knowledge of Catholicism. I think, T. S. Eliot is very religious. But is it right to call him ' Catholic Poet ' or so ? It is said that comparing Eliot with Auden, he seeks the way to religion from ' The Waste Land ', but Auden takes the way to Socialism. I think so, too.

Of course Eliot has the clear view about ' person and society '. In France, for instance, Francois Mauriac is called ' Catholic '.

But is it quite same Catholicism? (Maybe there is not two Catholicism, my question seems so silly.) I have opinion that Eliot and Mauriac is quite different—and this differency stands on their aims of literature.

Eliot wrote many short critics on 'Religion and Society'. I'll be so glad when I can understand what he thinks, and his attitude to the Religion.

Soon, the vacation will be over. Till the end of it, I have to make my direction of Study T. S. Eliot, I think.

If you have spare time, please tell me the name of few poet, novelist and author of Catholicism in England. I would like to know 'Catholicism' in English Literature.

Cool and wonderful Autumn will not come so soon. Please take care of yourself.

Excuse my hasty writing.

Yours Truly . . .

Her bewilderment on the point of Catholicism corresponds to the casual tourist's confusion between Buddhism and Shinto. But where he will go home next week and bluff it out, she has to write a thesis on T. S. Eliot. And then the charm of that last good wish—so feminine . . . For a moment one is tempted to shout 'Down with education, especially in foreign languages and literatures!' But that won't do—it is too late in the day. And so one reaches for one's pen, hoping not to add yet another misconception to the many which have vexed for so long the mutual relations of east and west.

3 : THE GREAT LEARNING

> ' Books should not be flung about, stridden
> over, or used as pillows. The corners
> should not be turned down, or spittle used
> to raise the leaves. If waste paper contains
> texts from the classics or the names of
> sages, boys should be careful not to apply
> it to common purposes. Nor should waste
> paper with the names of one's parents or
> lord be defiled.'
>
> (*From the Dōjikun of Kaibara Yekken, early
> eighteenth century, trans. W. G. Aston*)

IN 1940 there were forty-seven universities in Japan (including
Korea and Formosa) and the total enrolment of students was
51,439. Even then, it is said, there were more university
graduates than responsible jobs could be found for. The
sorting out of talent appears to have been largely prohibited
by the reluctance to distinguish publicly between the first-
rate and the second-rate. The Japanese would still find the
English system of first, second and third class degrees repug-
nant. John F. Embree writes of pre-war elementary schools
that ' practically all children are promoted every year, the
emphasis in teaching being as much on the ethics of human
relations as on the accumulation of knowledge. Teachers
feel that if some child were left behind his class he would feel
very much upset, and that the resulting psychological effect
and family chagrin would not be compensated for by any
good the child might receive from repeating the school grade.'
It is worthy of note that, by Embree's account, attention is
paid both to the individual (the child's feelings) and to
society (' the ethics of human relations '). But the psychology
of the argument is sound only if one assumes that chagrin
is inevitably a harmful experience.

41

Mr. Embree goes on to remark that ' at school athletic contests all entrants, not only the first three, receive prizes, so that no one feels unduly slighted '. The ' competitor ' knows that he has lost, he knows that everyone else knows, but he finds consolation in the fact that his defeat is not formally acknowledged. Is it a result of this careful sparing of feelings in youth, this external bolstering-up of a character which must know its own weaknesses, that the adult Japanese so often breaks down under reproach ? On one occasion in the local train a Japanese worker was requested by the conductor to conform with the regulations and extinguish his cigarette. The whole performance was exquisitely painful. To begin with, the official was so embarrassed that he put the request to the offender without halting in his progress through the train and almost without looking him in the face. But the spiritual condition of the offender was truly tormented. He stood up, smoked with energetic defiance until the conductor had passed into the next coach, stared through the window in an agony of self-consciousness, shifted from one foot to the other, grew more and more sullen-looking. At the next station he left the coach—I noticed that he walked down the platform and entered another coach where no one had witnessed his discomfiture. Leaving the terminal station I saw him again, blustering at a very mild ticket-collector. He was wrong, and he knew it, but . . . The Japanese are an obedient people who obey the rules and regulations : but if a rule should be broken, the spiritual consequences are intricate and painful for all concerned. There is no adequate apparatus for dealing with the ' unexpected '.

The humiliation of being asked in public to put out one's cigarette ? Surely this must have to do with the excessive precautions taken in early days to save feelings. It can be seen that, in the practice of these precautions, the Japanese knew all about democracy long before the Americans came. I am now awaiting the arrival of a few score examination papers. The pass-mark is sixty out of a hundred. When I asked roughly how many I could fail with impunity, I was told that those whom I failed would take the paper again and would then pass, so that, to save myself trouble, I should be well advised to pass them all the first time. And so everyone will get a prize.

If it was difficult for the brilliant person to declare himself under pre-war educational conditions, at least the universities could maintain their standards by taking off the cream of the country. The Imperial Universities, the Tokyo University of Education, Keio and Waseda and some others deserved their high reputations and their contribution to the speedy development of New Japan was enormous.[1] But after the war, in 1947, a new education law was passed at the instigation of a visiting American education mission. The principle of this law was that Japan pledged herself to ' foster an educational system aiming at the creation of universal culture and respecting the rights and needs of the individual '. It apparently did not occur to anyone that these two aims were not identical, that in fact they might be irreconcilable, and that anyway it was only the second that was essential at that moment in time. Consequently, after some form of ' screening ', the high schools were promoted to university status. And now, according to a recent count, there are 479 universities (counting the 252 *Tanki-Daigaku* or junior colleges which offer two-year courses), and total enrolment for the academic year April 1954 to March 1955 is estimated at roughly 600,000. Both the number of universities and the number of students are now ten times what they were fourteen years ago. A university degree, that is to say, has become a minimum requirement, corresponding to the General Certificate of Education in England, though perhaps under the present difficult conditions of rather less value than that piece of paper. It is ironical that this departure from pre-war

---

[1] Among other Englishmen who have taught at these universities are Edmund Blunden, Ralph Hodgson, Sherard Vines, Peter Quennell, William Empson, John Morris, George Barker and G. S. Fraser. William Plomer taught for a time at a high school in Tokyo.

tradition, the least healthy of all the Occupation measures, should be the only one not now abolished or ' corrected '. The *zaibatsu* (the big combines) are reappearing—according to some critics, both Japanese and American, they never really disappeared—the police are being un-decentralized, and the Japanese people are being asked kindly to renounce their renunciation of war. But so far ' democratic education ' remains intact. Why ? Because it has become a *zaibatsu* itself ?

The ensuing state of affairs is so confused that I cannot understand it well enough to describe it coherently. The big pre-war universities still retain a prestige value, and therefore intending students will first of all take the entrance examinations of these institutions. It is said that yearly applications for these examinations average eight times the actual capacity in the case of Tokyo (Imperial) University and twelve times in that of Waseda University. Unsuccessful candidates will then rush on to take the entrance examination at their second choice, and so forth down the list—by an act of mercy examination dates are staggered so that the student has ample opportunity to exhaust himself before entering upon his academic career. It will be seen that since a university education is absolutely imperative, the many new universities, ' private ' as distinct from central or local government institutions, are assured of clients even though they may lack intellectual prestige. It will also be seen that, since they are business concerns, they may be tempted to accept more students than they can properly cater for. Sad to say, it appears that some of them have succumbed to this temptation.

According to an article in the Japanese *Sankei Weekly*, Chūō University accepted in April 1954 twice as many students as the school was supposed to hold. The 19,122 candidates for the entrance examination paid a fee of ¥2,000 (£2), and each of the 5,640 successful ones had to meet the following charges :

Admittance fee . . .	¥6,000
Tuition fee	¥20,000
Equipment charge . .	¥6,000
Sundries	¥1,000

—thus the university received some 225 million yen. The same article reports that Nippon University made 746 million yen by accepting twice as many students as it could accommodate—this sum representing 70 per cent of the total annual expenses incurred by the university in the provision of its four-year courses. Where do the profits go ? Certainly not into the pockets of the teachers. Moreover, it is said that every university asks for a donation of at least ¥10,000 on enrolment for improvement of facilities, while in several cases the student takes out a life insurance policy with his university as the beneficiary. Japanese newspapers are apt to go in for sensationalism [1]—there is always plenty of material available—but all the same it surprises the foreign reader to find an article on institutions of learning which ends with this sentence : ' One is asked to rely on the " conscience " of private school administrators. But have they a " conscience " is the question ? '

We have mentioned the academic and the business aspects of Japanese universities. In connection with the former we should note that even in pre-war days there was nothing corresponding to our tutorial system. While the relationship between master and pupil remains as formal as it is, there is no possibility of introducing that system, even if the numbers of students were sufficiently low. It is partly owing to this deplorable lack of guidance that students are so pathetically vulnerable to such insidious foreign fashions as Wastelanditis

[1] The Press, that is to say, is making the most of its freedom. The leading newspaper, the *Asahi Shimbun*, has an excellent reputation—it fell foul of the militarists during the war and, less seriously, of the Occupation authorities afterwards. Today it keeps a keen eye open for any signs of backsliding, and its power is such that one cannot easily imagine it yielding to improper political pressures. Japanese reporters are a little overpowering. But if Mr. Bevan had had any genuine interest in the country he was visiting he would not have complained, as he is said to have done, that ' there are too many newspaper-men in Japan '.

and Existentializing—that is, to their own half-baked versions of those fashions. In the course of an evening one such young man led off with a question about Existentialism. As we were not in a *sensei* mood—in fact we were harmlessly engaged on a tasty supper of grilled eels and rice—I attempted to avert the storm by assuring him that, as for myself, existence was quite enough to get along with. The young man then turned to my wife, to tell her that he was especially interested in the poets of the French Resistance because he felt that resistance was precisely what Japan needed today. Resistance against what, my wife asked, against the American 'occupation'? The Japanese gentleman who was perforce interpreting for us—he happened to be the original of 'Kyo Gisors' in Malraux's *La Condition Humaine*—looked as pained as if he had swallowed his chopsticks. 'No,' he informed us, 'the young man says that he is not thinking of the Americans. He says that he means resistance against oneself. . . .' 'Kyo' sighed deeply; he had been with the Maquis and had a proper respect for words. 'Mental indigestion,' he remarked to us later, 'the great complaint of Japan. . . . It's all this Zen that's at the bottom of it.' And of course today's student is tomorrow's *sensei* and the state of affairs degenerates further. It is certainly a powerful argument for those who would like to see 'Japanese Thought' reinstalled, along with the Thought Police to protect everybody from mental indigestion. Those intellectuals who treasure their freedom are betraying their cause by ranting in the magazines when they should be striving to correct this mental anarchy before it swings over into tyranny.[1]

In connection with the second aspect, the business side, it is clear that while a degree is a necessary qualification for an office stool then money will be made out of providing it. What we should better be considering is not academic stand-

[1] The present situation is indeed a far cry from the early years of the century when, as an Englishwoman then resident in Japan tells us, ' Japanese translations of Molière's works have been suppressed by common consent simply because they ridiculed old age.'

ards or business morality but the actual conditions of student life. This can most simply be done by summarizing the informative and moving documentary film, *Today's Students, Japan's Tomorrow*, made by Francis Haar with the help of students from Kyoto and Dōshisha universities.

'Matsumoto' is the younger son of a country family. Their patch of land is not large enough to support him, and he persuades his father to let him go to the university. Scholarships, in the English sense, do not exist in Japan.[1] So he works as a domestic servant, which leaves him little time for study. He changes to a milk round, and then to a job in a printing shop, where he is distressed by the seditious political talk of his mates. Some of his friends are selling their blood to meet expenses : Matsumoto looks as if he has very little to spare.[2] We see him next as a dishwasher. But there comes a time when Matsumoto has to remember that after all students are supposed to study. A brief shot of a geography lecture in progress—'Japan's population : 226 to the square kilometre '—makes an important point here ; especially when we add that only 15 per cent of Japan's surface area is cultivated, as compared with 85 per cent in England and 60 per cent in America. And so we watch Matsumoto pawning his overcoat and scarf. (Kyoto is a bleak place in winter.) The proceeds pay for a few bowls of noodles. But books are out of the question. University libraries appear to be reserved for the use of the staff, and students must queue for hours to get into the big municipal libraries. For books

---

[1] Grants of about ¥2,000 (£2) per month are made available to approximately a third of the student body by the Japanese Scholarship Association.

[2] Extract from a letter to the *Asahi Shimbun*, Tokyo, written by a student : ' The other day I went to the office of a blood transfusion society. What surprised me was that all of the students present there had the type of pallid and swollen faces usually found in persons who are undernourished. I was told that each of these students sells 3,000 cubic centimetres of blood a month on the average.' The price paid is 10s. per 100 c.c.

Matsumoto drops into a bookshop to do his reading on the spot. There is a shot of the bookseller searching along the shelves for a customer's request. We know that it is the book which Matsumoto is deep in. There is an effective little scene as the bookseller slowly prizes it out of the student's reluctant hands : a show of precarious politeness all round and, underneath, the bookseller's irritation and the student's bitter resentment. The film tells us a good deal about modern Japan quite apart from the lot of students.

Matsumoto falls sick : his lungs are affected. His friend Mitsuko, an attractive girl student, makes up her mind to take a job, secretly, in a tea-shop, to earn money for his medical expenses. Is this an attempt to work a little romantic interest into a bleak documentary? It seems like that— until we recognize Mitsuko, carrying a tray, dressed in a ridiculously short skirt, suddenly very plain and pathetically bandy-legged. Yes, one seems to have seen that—it is authentic. Finally other students come to the rescue and enough money is collected to send Matsumoto to hospital. We are content not to ask what happens after that.

So much for the film. In case Francis Haar should have let his artistic feeling run away with him, let us look at the statistics. Firstly, more than 300,000 university students in Japan must work in order to cover part of their expenses, and more than 50,000 of these must earn the whole. Secondly, *The Japanese Student News Service* (issue No. 5, 31 December 1953) states that Kyoto University Welfare Consultative Council sent out 703 health questionnaires to students of that university, and 228 replies were received. Of these, 159 (i.e. 70 per cent) admitted to sickness, and it transpired that 138 were suffering from T.B. Investigation revealed that— as the film implied—most of the patients had discovered the nature of their illness only after it had reached a serious stage. Japanese students often look healthier than they really are (just as the Japanese people in general look less poor than they are, much to the comfort of the tourists and the well-to-do foreign residents), but the effects show when they reach their

1. High School Girls, Kyūshū.

2. 'Paper Theatre': the story-teller with his coloured slides.

thirties. The sheer will-power, the obstinate tenacity, for which the nation is famous—and, through the last war, notorious—is strong in the student. It too often takes the place of a square meal and medical attention.

Today's Students, Japan's Tomorrow ended with the remark that it had no solution to offer, but believed that the presentation of the problem was the first step towards finding a solution. It is hoped to exhibit the film in England. In England there are greater efforts being made to provide common rooms than there are in Japan to provide hospital beds for consumptive undergraduates. English students might like to know how their Japanese contemporaries are growing up.

The foregoing pages may have suggested that the industry and application of the Japanese student are merely a response to the employment situation and the necessity of acquiring a degree. That is not so. He is by nature, as well as by circumstance, earnest and hard-working. Whether this characteristic dates back no further than the opening of Japan to the west and the sudden realization of how much there was to be learnt, I do not know. From 1870 onwards Smiles's *Self-Help* was a best-seller in Japan. And today one has the overwhelming impression that a mass of people are driven by the urge of self-improvement. To learn—whether the thing learnt is useful or useless, important or trivial, does not always seem to matter. The poems of Ralph Hodgson will be explicated with the same thoroughness as those of Gerard Manley Hopkins. The words of a foreign visitor will be hung upon with gratifying attentiveness just as soon as he makes known his willingness to pronounce. I am always moved afresh by this zeal for knowledge, and by the gratitude with which the Japanese receive the most insignificant pieces of information (such as the fact that the British Isles are not subject to typhoons but are acquainted with thunderstorms), and disturbed by the uncritical attitude which they often display towards oracles from abroad. Publish a poem in an

D

English parish magazine, let the fact be known in Japan, and you stand a good chance of being accepted as a considerable English poet. On the other hand, admit to a fondness for feminine company or an occasional drink and you may find yourself acquiring the reputation of a whoremonger or a drunk. It is temperance that is generally missed from Japan's attitude towards the west; and it has seemed to me something of a duty—in so far as I have felt any duty at all—to insist that the crows in the west are roughly as black as those in the east and the snow is roughly as white. One of the greatest deterrents to writing this book has been the fact that, in spite of a mass of literature in several languages, Japan's misconceptions about the west are only exceeded by the west's misconceptions about Japan.

While writing the first draft of this chapter I had one ear on the radio. Dr. Summerskill, one of the Labour Party Delegation, was addressing a public meeting in Tokyo. She pointed out in a clipped and acerb tone of voice that there were about two hundred and fifty men present to every woman. She also pointed out that democracy meant equal rights for men and women, which implied allowing your wife to take a job outside the home if she had any talent in that direction. Dr. Summerskill did not propose any course of action for the men who would then be put out of work; it did not strike her that a number of employed men were already redundant and that to add female redundancy to male redundancy would hardly be a happy demonstration of democracy. With a good deal of ingenuity she then praised Japan for giving equal pay to male and female teachers—' a reform which we in England have not yet achieved '. (Applause.) It did not strike her that the purchasing power of a male teacher's salary is so meagre that it would hardly be feasible to pay less to a female. The Japanese have a proverb about ' a bee stinging a weeping face '. And Dr. Summerskill is an educated woman and an M.P., and not a mere tourist.

Some students frequent missionary meetings, not to absorb

the teaching of Christ, but to improve their English by listening to the voice of the preacher. English and American publications are beyond the means of all but a few, but the bookshops are rich in Communist literature, books and magazines written in English, and sold at low prices to students who are keen to extend their knowledge not of Marx but of the English language. It is not surprising, then, that many Japanese, young and old, attend the cinema in part for its educational value. Being nice-minded, they lack the cynicism which might deter them from swallowing Hollywood, Elstree or Paris wholesale. It was in the course of the same day that I found myself first of all warning a Japanese scholar that England was not entirely like the technicolour publicity film he had just seen of Buckingham Palace and Stratford-on-Avon, and later pleading with another and rather horrified Japanese not to believe that *La Ronde* was a faithful account of French family life. The only solution is that exchange of persons—and not only of books and films and politicians and business men—should be more common between Japan and the west. The finances of the British Council prevent it from doing more than a little in this direction; and its small staff in Tokyo is desperately struggling to satisfy the enormous demands of a whole country, increasing on all fronts from day to day. If we could arrive at the position where every comparatively respectable university and if possible some of the high schools had one member of staff who had passed a year or two in England, then it would be more than the teaching of English which would be clarified. And if England could send more teachers to Japan, to teach and to learn, the process would be speeded up. At present, of course, America is sending a number of teachers (some of them serious but many of them rather light-weight) on two-year contracts with Japanese universities. And Japan is sending some of her national arts, adapted for the dollar market, in exchange—but that is material for a separate chapter.

What I wish to stress is that, contrary to the opinion of many foreigners, the Japanese desire to learn from abroad is sincere and deep-seated. It may not always be very critical, it may seize on the wrong end of the stick, but it is not mere snobbism. The enthusiasm for western (i.e. ' serious ') music is a case in point. Anything more different from traditional Japanese music it would be hard to imagine, whether by western music you mean Bach, Berg or Tchaikovsky. The best Japanese orchestras are probably not up to the standard of the best European or American, but they are good, and the broadcasting companies devote generous time to them and to recordings of foreign musicians—except when base-ball intervenes. The foreign performer can depend on full houses in Japan, even though he may not always get them at home. Mr. Morris remarks that ' long before the war the sale of Beethoven recordings in Japan was higher than in any other country ' (which today might possibly be true of volumes by T. S. Eliot and Herbert Read). This calls up another point : that Japanese of very moderate or even, by our standards, low incomes are prepared to spend a consider-able sum regularly on recordings and more particularly on books. Snobbism usually contrives to borrow other people's purchases.

For the foreigner many of the excellent broadcast concerts are spoilt by the announcer who insists on describing the music even after it has started. Once, after a surfeit of the *samisen*, that touching but so sad music, I went to a gramo-phone recital of Sibelius's Second Symphony at the local American Cultural Centre. But alas it too was instructional. An austere and scholarly-looking Japanese talked throughout the performance, giving details of the composer's life, ex-horting his listeners to watch out for the repetition of some particular theme, urging upon them the fact that in so many minutes' time the horns would be entering or departing. Sibelius is a powerful composer, but he couldn't make himself heard above the din of explication. The members of the audience, however, were contentedly scribbling down the commentator's words. On another occasion I heard a radio programme of popular French *chansons*—currently all the rage here—in which two-thirds of the time was used by the commentator earnestly explaining such cruces as 'Place Pigalle' and 'Bohemian'. All this makes one feel that one belongs to a very old and decadent civilization.

All the same, this urge to learn can take strange forms and it sometimes carries unhappy implications. '.Ballet of late,' states an article in the *Yomiuri Weekly*, 'has become in Japan an accomplishment "absolutely necessary" for marriage for girls, like the tea ceremony and flower arrangement.' (One wonders, incidentally, whether the pirouette and the *pas de deux* will accrete the same aura of philosophical significance as attaches to the other two cults mentioned.) The consequence is that about a thousand little ballet studios have shot up in Tokyo. A Japanese ballet critic explains the phenomenon in this way : 'These people who start ballet studies generally take up the art under some well-known ballet dancers for half a year or so. When they have acquired the ABC, they leave their teachers and before you know it you see their names in the sign of a new ballet school they have founded with the aid of a patron—what kind of patron, it's up to you to guess.'

The urge to learn is so great that anyone who has taken a few lessons can set up as a professor ; the boom in ballet studios is simply part of the general boom in education. There are always students, students and more students—that well never runs dry. And one can only suppose that they are all so *sensei*-conscious, so respectful and so nice-minded that the teacher is able to get away with murder. One has heard of so many foreign missionaries who are described as 'great teachers' of English literature that one can well believe that Tokyo contains a thousand 'great teachers' of ballet.

All well and good. But then the article goes on to mention that not even one of the professional ballet troupes in the country is free from grave financial difficulties. Masahide Komaki, leader of the best-known company in Japan, is said to be £4,000 in debt. How does this happen ? It has to be granted that Mr. Komaki himself, perhaps the most famous male dancer here, is a curiously wooden performer, and that his troupe as a whole are conspicuously lacking in *brio* and control.   But even so, with all this enthusiasm for ballet . . . But the enthusiasm is not exactly for ballet ; it is for learning, for teaching.   Here, as in certain other Japanese pursuits, the means is not justified by the end—it is the end.   I am reminded of the student, now in his final year, whose firm intention it is to be a linguist and a university teacher.   The fact that at present he is hardly capable of speaking six consecutive words in any foreign tongue will not deter him, and he would consider me a vulgar materialist if I expressed any doubts about the fitness of his ambitions.   Not that I intend to do so, for in a few years, unless he is unlucky, he will be a *sensei* specializing in that greatest of all means without an end, Language.

Perhaps the only way in which one can write a truly smooth and orderly book on a foreign country is by abjuring the company of the people you are writing about.   Then one can achieve those neat and tidy chapters on Thought, Behaviour, Art, and Attitudes.   Such, at least, must be my face-saver for the dishevelled appearance of this collection of impressions.

It was immediately after jotting down notes on the popularity of western ' serious ' music that I met several senior newspaper and radio men who told me unanimously that, on reaching the middle forties, their taste for foreign music and art and food suddenly collapsed.   From Beethoven they turned back with relief to *naga-uta* (literally, ' long poems ') and *naniwabushi* (dramatic recitations to musical accompaniment) ; from Ibsen-in-translation to *bunraku*, the puppet theatre (a very sensible preference in my opinion) ; from Picasso and Rouault to the Japanese artists of *kakemono* and screen ; from whiskey to *sake*, the rice-wine.   Their remarks deserve to be stated, but I should hesitate to draw any deductions from them.   Tired business men are not representative of much apart from other tired business men.   And more-

over, the gentleman who was most definite about this return
to ' things Japanese ' was drinking Scotch the while and ended
by kindly inviting me to accompany him to the new theatre
in Osaka specially built to house something called the O.S.
Nude Show, for which he had conceived a considerable
enthusiasm. One cannot think of many things less ' Japanese ' than strip-tease (' sŭtorippu ')—or of anything less
seductive than the short-legged small-breasted Japanese strip-
dancer throwing off her garments as if she were in a hurry
to jump into the public bath. Yet the O.S. Nude Show has
arrived ; and its clientele, my informant said, consists of
middle-aged Japanese gentlemen with a generous sprinkling
of foreigners. Charming as Japanese music can be, it is
remarkably narrow and predictable in emotional range. And
the phenomenon described is perhaps less a return to ' things
Japanese ' than a relapse to things easier on the brain.

The Japanese student will rarely be seen in such a place.
For one thing he is usually hard-up. For another, he is
inclined to be puritanical. On first arriving in Japan I
offered a cigarette to one of my students, a well-to-do and
presentable young man. He refused sternly on the grounds
that smoking among ' young people ' led to juvenile delin-
quency. And once I gave a beer party for a group of students
—an emergency call for orange juice was sent out and I
drank the beer myself.

The interesting question is—what do today's students
really think, and how will they develop ? Will they too
relapse into ' things Japanese ', that attitude of mind which
often implies complacency about social conditions, a blind
resolve to hold on to what one has and to pass it on to one's
eldest son when he has finished sowing his intellectual wild
oats at the university and in the cinema ? I cannot believe
that this will be the case. The situation of the young Japanese is—it seems worth repeating—peculiarly difficult. When
students talk to me of ' the war which our militarists forced
us into ', I know that they are wholly sincere. The war-
repudiating constitution was welcome to them, even though

it was imposed from without. There was nothing hypocritical about their acceptance of it. And now the war-
repudiating constitution has been taken away from them—
and, to make matters more confusing, taken away from
outside. For few of them would agree that Mr. Yoshida
and his government are 'inside' the country. To soothe
them, their statesmen tell them that Japan's national pride
demands that she should have an army.

And so the wheel has come full circle. At least in the
eyes of some of the politicians it has come full circle. The
students, however, and the mass of the people have not
followed it round. They became giddy and fell off some time
ago. Japan's reaction to the Bikini H-bomb test could
hardly have been more violent had the bomb fallen on Tokyo.
Yet, in its context, their dismay and indignation are understandable. First the atom bombs, then capitulation, then
liberation from feudal restrictions and the promise of eternal
peace (along of course with extreme national poverty and a
good deal of sheer physical suffering). And then suddenly
this 'progress'—and I think that for once the word was
accurate—came to an official end. A National Safety Force
was instituted, which in July 1954 grew into the Self-Defence
Forces, a rose by two other names ; plans for social security
improvements were put aside in favour of rearmament ; the
suicide rate rose (2·3 per 10,000 yearly) ; and, the hardest
cut of all, the Americans dropped a hydrogen bomb which
claimed Japanese fishermen as its first victims. The men
who had silently opposed the new constitution must have
had a good laugh—both at the Americans, who were having
to undo what they had done, and at their own countrymen,
with their pathetic dreams of a little peace and a little happiness. It is no wonder that some of the students, some of
Matsumoto's colleagues, should have turned to Communism,
feeling that they had been thoroughly betrayed by every
other system of thought.

In spite of the confusion in which the student is growing
up, I have faith in his ability—if total war can be averted,

of course—to make a better Japan. A student of mine
wrote : ' Some say that the old family system was a beautiful
custom unique and original in Japan. But I dare say that
that system was a hot-bed of insularism and that the selfish
concern for one's own family alone prevented us from taking
any interest in or care of other families. Do you think it
a beautiful custom ? We should not restore the old traditional family system, but we should set up the dignity of the
individual and keep the principle of equality. And thus
create a family system with a new significance, in which we
can learn self-respect and confidence as well as social responsibility and communal co-operation. In which we can
breed all-round personalities who will work in agreement and
harmony for the betterment of our society.' I do not think
that this was a mere exercise in English language.

And then it was a girl student in a well-known Tokyo
women's college whose formal aim is character-building based
on Christian principles that began a report for me thus :
' In Japan, few years ago, Lawrence's best novel, *Lady
Chatterley's Lover*, was taken into court. I remember that
was for no reason than it is obscenity. Many people bought
it but this is a question whether it was read correctly by
them. I am going to hurry to know Lawrence in this chance.'
Will she relapse into ' Japanese womanliness ' ? Another
student of the same college summed up the William-Anna
relationship in *The Rainbow* in this vivid and economical
fashion : ' Now then, they began to have flaming consum-
mating sexual communion. But again they come to the
" Darkness and death of their own sensual activities ". So
William takes up Ecclesiastical woodwork, and playing organ
for the outlet of darkness of soul, while his wife is buried in
breeding a dozen of children.' I know the young lady and,
even when we allow for the swashbuckling element in adoles-
cence, I cannot really think that she is going to turn into a
quiet little woman ' buried in breeding a dozen of children '.
In the past the ' new woman ' has been a rather scandalous
joke, but there are too many of them now, and too many

informed young men, for the traditionalists to have it all their own way. The Japanese student knows that he has little in the way of comfort to expect from the immediate future, whatever may happen in the world at large. But he also knows that his country is too far committed to western conceptions of moral equality, personal responsibility and social conscience to be able to retreat. Although the Americans soon pulled down the blind, the people have seen what was displayed in the shop window—and they want some of it.

On my first day in Japan one of my future pupils came up to me looking intensely worried—an expression which I have since become accustomed to. 'We do not know what to call you,' he blurted out. 'Call me what you like, within limits.' 'Might we . . . could we,' he asked timidly, 'call you " sir " ? ' 'By all means—why not ? ' (After all, ' sir ' is a more neutral title than *sensei*; and somehow or other the latter is rarely bestowed upon foreign teachers, I suspect.) 'Well, sir,' he explained in a relieved tone, 'the Americans told us that we should not call anybody " sir ".'

4 : THE ANCIENT POND

Gods have bestowed our genius on us ;
They will also find its use some day . . .
(Li Po, trans. Shigeyoshi Obata)

SUCH has been the tenacity of ancient poetic form that the revolutionary event of 1882, the *Shintaishishō* or ' Poetry of New Form ', consisted of Japanese versions of Bloomfield, Campbell (' The Mariners of England '), Tennyson (' The Charge of the Light Brigade '), Gray, Longfellow, Charles Kingsley and Shakespeare. In these translations, moreover, the traditional alternation of phrases of five and seven syllables was retained. Shimazaki Tōson, who was considered to be the first major poet of the ' New Style ' and who died in 1943, achieved his first success at the end of the last century with ' Song of the Autumn Wind ', a piece noticeably indebted to Shelley and far removed from the *fin de siècle* tendencies of Europe. But Japanese poets have now caught up. Indeed, a poem written in 1909 by Kitahara Hakushū, an early ' symbolist ', contains the proleptically surrealist line, ' my sorrow wears the thin flannel garb of one-sided love '. And now, helped by the ravages of the war and the bitter confusion of post-war, they have even overtaken the rest of us as far as despair, horror and the sense of ruin are concerned. The rats' alley, the falling tower and the landscape of broken tombstones feature prominently in contemporary Japanese verse, along with the atom bomb which after all is a part of the Japanese scene and provides more justification for this kind of imagery than western poets have had.[1]

Something of this kind had to happen, I think. Where English poetry consists of waves of action and reaction,

[1] See p. 205.

Japanese poetry resembles rather a steady continuous flow between narrow banks. Nowhere in that past could the modern Japanese poet find a foot-hold from which he could launch himself; for him there was nothing that could have the kind of significance which the seventeenth century had for our moderns. Life had changed so suddenly: the delicate and conventionalized images of blossom, mountain and moon were suddenly inept in a world of factory chimneys, electric railways and bombers. Even in the west the jolt was savage, as the note of self-consciousness in *The Waste Land* and the occasional exaggeration of its imagery might suggest. In Japan it was immeasurably more violent, and the jolt persisted into a clash, for the old traditions, instead of meekly dying away, endured in the least expected places.

The traditional Japanese poem is based formally upon the alternation of five and seven syllable phrases, innocent of both rhyme and metre. Thus the *tanka* comprises thirty-one syllables arranged in 'lines' of 5, 7, 5, 7 and 7 syllables, while the *haiku*, a form extremely popular since its introduction in the early sixteenth century, takes the shape of a *tanka* without its final 'couplet' and is only seventeen syllables in length. The bar touts, who strive to inveigle passers, and particularly foreign devils, into their establishments at all hours of the day and night, might seem to have nothing in common with poetic studies. But one of the many invitation cards pressed into my hand in Kobe reads thus (on the back is a useful map in Japanese and English):

SERVICES BY CHARMING GIRLS

The days ! worries will be gone
When at the BAR SEA-QUEEN a
night aspent is done,
With fair nice pretty girls, all
Waiting forever eagerly for your
call.

Counting will show that the writer, though no great poet, has felt the instinctive urge to obey the 7–5 alternation.

Unfortunately his attempts to supply the alien commodity of rhyme and the fact that there is so much to say about the girls prove too much for him and his *tanka* jumps off the rails.

The remarks which follow should not be taken too seriously, since the author can claim no authority whatsoever where Japanese literature is concerned. The most I can say is that I have read fairly widely in various translations of Japanese poetry, alongside the romanization of the original, and with a Japanese scholar to point out the word-play and the diversity of interpretation. Such a reading, it must be confessed, is disappointing. Too often the only feeling provoked in my perhaps cynical breast is ' So what ? '

Some Japanese authorities have taken violent exception to the suggestion by foreign scholars that *tanka* are ' given over to small fancies wrought under lyric impulse ' and at least one of them has demanded that *tanka* should be likened rather to Shakespeare's sonnets and the shorter poems of Words-worth and Keats. Even on the face of it I cannot find this very likely. We need only think of English poetry if it had been dominated by one form, say the sonnet, with the con-sequent loss of such variety of genius as we have between Pope and Keats or George Herbert and W. B. Yeats. Even when one has allowed for the fact that English, with its tendency to stress if not to rhyme, is hardly the language in which to convey the allusive and deliberately modest spirit of *tanka* and *haiku*, one may still wonder whether Japanese scholars can without prior knowledge distinguish between the productions of one of their great poets and those of another. With the isolated and even insulated, short-lived and sensitive expression of mood the Japanese are thoroughly at home. They rarely moralize, and thus their poetry is saved from the worst excesses of western platitudinousness : there is never any suggestion of bathos, since the tone of the poem has never led the reader to expect any notable pro-fundity. Or, one should perhaps rather say, any explicit profundity. It was this characteristic which recommended

haiku to the English and American Imagist poets—and it
certainly helped them to get away from late-Victorian
turgidity.

The sad thing—as it seems to me—is that the Japanese
poets have not been reacting against anything. And that
very freedom from moralizing seems in the end to have
constituted an actual bondage—the bondage of artifice—and
to have led to a loss of contact with what we call ' society '.
The *tanka* or *haiku* is the poem of a man alone—but is it
the poem of an individual ? Probably we in the west think
too much about the audience and about ' social responsibility ' ; but it seems to me that the poet who is interested
neither in society nor in his own individuality might find a
more amenable function in either a monastery or a Department of Philosophy. It is significant that the great mass of
scholarship attached to traditional Japanese poetry consists of
interpretation, of filling in the putative background and in
pointing out allusions and ambiguities, rather than in critical
evaluation. The Japanese poet Yone Noguchi wrote, ' I
deem it one of the literary fortunes, a happy happening, but
not an achievement, that till quite recently our Japanese
poetry was never annoyed, fatigued, tormented by criticism ;
it was left perfectly at liberty to pursue its own free course
and satisfy its old sweet will.' [1] And indeed there seems to
be little for the critic as such to get a grip on. Noguchi
remarked, apropos of Tennyson and Swinburne, ' My own
Japanese mind already revolts and rebels against something
in English poems or verses which, for lack of a proper expression, we might call physical or external. As my attention
is never held by the harmony of language, I go straight-
forward to the writer's inner soul to speculate on it, and talk
with it . . . our Japanese minds always turn, let me dare say,

[1] *The Spirit of Japanese Poetry*, London, 1914. These passages
from the book are certainly illuminating but, although Noguchi
speaks of his ' Japanese mind ', I doubt whether many living
Japanese writers would wish to be identified with him as either a
writer about poetry or a writer of poetry.

to something imaginative.' Style, in the European sense of the word, is rarely the subject of discussion. '*Le style c'est l'homme*': most Japanese poetry appears to be anonymous. Perhaps it is rude, perhaps it is 'unexpected', to be different, to put yourself forward. I once asked some colleagues how they could tell a good *haiku* from a bad one. 'We cannot,' replied one of them, 'the trouble is that we don't know what standards to apply. But perhaps you, from Cambridge . . .' He smiled politely. Another suggested with a strangled cough, 'All *haiku* are good, perhaps?' I am still wondering what exactly both of them meant.

As examples of *haiku* in English dress, I quote several by the two poets held to be the greatest masters of the form. They seem to me typical and at the same time more than usually meaningful. The first three, all of them classical examples, are by Bashō (1644–94):

> The ancient pond
> A frog leaps in
> The sound of the water.

> On the withered branch
> A crow has alighted—
> The end of autumn.

> Such stillness—
> The cries of the cicadas
> Sink into the rocks.[1]

The following three are by Buson (1716–84):

> A flash of lightning !
> The sound of drops
> Falling among the bamboos.

---

[1] These three translations by Dr. Donald Keene come from his *Japanese Literature : An Introduction for Western Readers*, London, 1953.

With the evening breeze,
The water laps against
The heron's legs.

The scissors hesitate
Before the white chrysanthemums,
A moment.[1]

Mr. Blyth implies that in his opinion the vagueness of the
Japanese language is a positive virtue : ' There is in life no
fixed subject and predicate, cause and effect. . . . Things
do not begin with a capital letter and end with a full stop ;
there is simply ceaseless becoming. The English language
does not recognize this ; hence the chief difficulty of the
translator.' Well, yes, but art after all is art ; it is the achieved
and not the ceaseless becoming. And while the Japanese
dispense with that capital letter and that full stop which to
some of us may seem to be of the essence of art, they do all
the same carry with them the atmosphere of a most contrived,
sometimes even precious, artistry. I have heard Japanese
themselves complain that Japanese thinking is debilitated by
a certain lack of continuity or progression. (It is in their
will-power that persistence features, and will-power has kept
them going where logical thought—the pushing to its conclusion of a line of reasoning—would have resulted in revolution or collapse.) I think that it is in this point that the
real cause of our dissatisfaction with Japanese poetry lies.
My favourite *haiku* is the one by Moritake (1472–1549) :

A fallen flower
Returning to the branch ?
It was a butterfly.[2]

It is fresh and vivid ; it seems to me (though one Japanese
writer considered it rather crude and obvious) to represent
the short Japanese poem at the summit of its potentialities.

[1] Translated by Mr. R. H. Blyth and included in his book, *Haiku*
(Vol. I, *Eastern Culture*).　　　　[2] Trans. R. H. Blyth.

3. *Kabuki :* 'Kanjinchō', with Matsumoto Kōshirō, centre, as Benkei

4. *Kabuki :* 'Kagami Jishi', the late Kikugorō VI as the Lion.

Yet wouldn't we expect it to be *part* of a poem rather than a poem in itself? It is not a plea for *length* in poetry that I am making, but a plea for humanity. There seems to be a self-conscious casualness about the Japanese poet—as if he were a sort of dilettante, picking up an image here and an image there, but quickly dropping them again. One hardly has time to get one's mental fingers around the poem before it has gone. There is certainly no room, even in the *naga-uta*, the so-called 'long poem', for a powerful line of the nature of ' But Love has pitched his mansion in / The place of excrement' (though one might find a debased version of it in some of the popular songs) or ' That dolphin-torn, that gong-tormented sea.'

Was Mr. Clay MacCauley's word ' fancies ' so inappropriate, after all ? Isn't Fancy—as distinct from Imagination—exactly what Japanese poetry excels in expressing? ' Fancy ' is always short-winded, whereas ' Imagination ' takes longer to get into its stride than *tanka* or *haiku* permit, for ' Imagination ' implies the application of the poem to humanity, and that requires continuity and development. In a temple in Kyoto there is an old screen drawing of a tree. Age has blurred its outlines, but originally, the guide will tell you, there was a bird perched on the tree. It was so realistic that one day it flew away, out of the picture. ' There, you see,' he says triumphantly, ' it is not there ! ' Japanese poetry is rather similar—so sensitive and so profound that the bird of humanity has flown away. The Blake commentator mentioned in the next chapter denied that the *Songs of Innocence* had anything to do with children—that would have condemned them to triviality. But it takes a foreign enthusiast, attempting to deny his own blood, to put the matter really clearly : ' There is a Buddhist text which truly declares that he alone is wise *who can see things without their individuality*. And it is this Buddhist way of seeing which makes the greatness of the true Japanese art.' [1]

It is significant that Chinese poetry has been so much more

[1] *Kokoro*, by Lafcadio Hearn, 1896.

E

successfully translated into English; and, moreover, by the
same translator. Arthur Waley's Li Po and Po Chü-i can
be read with the critical attention one would give to good
original English poetry: that attention will remain in abey-
ance when we read his versions of *uta* or of *Nō*. Similarly,
Ezra Pound's *Nō* plays, though they have a certain exotic
interest, are not in the same class as his *Cathay*. The Japanese
translator, Shigeyoshi Obata, has turned Li Po into excellent
English verse and was also partly responsible for the English
version of the *Manyōshū*, the famous anthology completed
in the early ninth century, published by the Nippon Gaku-
jutsu Shinkōkai in 1940. But though the latter volume
contains the best translations of *Manyōshū* poems which I
have seen, there are few pieces in it which can compare for
impact with Li Po. The Japanese say that Chinese food
is for the stomach whereas Japanese food is for the eyes.
Perhaps that difference extends to the poetry of the two
nations—Chinese poetry is 'meaty' while Japanese is predominantly vegetarian.

One thing which I find very difficult to believe is that the
Japanese language, when used for poetic purposes, requires
by its very nature the alternation of five- and seven-syllable
phrases. Living languages are generally pliable; and as far
as the adoption and adaptation of foreign words and phrases
is concerned, there is no language which displays more fervour
than the Japanese at the present time. And whether or not
the Japanese 'modernists' have yet produced any indubitably
great verse, it seems to me altogether creditable that they are
not prostrating themselves before the old tyranny of the
miniature and the remote.

I have mentioned elsewhere that fortunate custom whereby
the Japanese, having fenced themselves in with a rigid set of
conventions, remember to make a few concessions to the old
Adam. Something of that nature has happened with regard
to the *haiku*. And the 'relaxation' takes the shape of the
senryū, an unedifying, earthy and satirical little poem, identical
in form with the *haiku*; it originated in the eighteenth century

with the poet Karai Hachiemon, whose pen-name was Senryū. Mr. Blyth has indulged in the translation of *senryū* as a relaxation from his concern with *haiku* and Zen, and I recommend to anyone who can get hold of a copy his amusing and charmingly illustrated collection.[1] The *senryū* is as short-winded as the *haiku*, and it is not always pointed. But at least it manages to contend with vulgar and undignified situations, whether of this kind :

> The barber washes his hands
>> Over the head of the person
> Whose hair he is washing.

or this, where 'she' is a prostitute :

> After the parting of lovers,
>> She has a nap,
> Alone.

It can make a critical point about the mechanical nature of much *tanka* writing by commenting on how the five syllables of the Japanese word for cuckoo set us hunting for the rest of the integer :

> ' *Hototogisu* ',
>> Makes us think
> Of twenty-six more syllables.

It can be shrewd, about the daughter

>> Showing her mother
>> The letter
> From a man she doesn't like.

And rather bitter, as in this reflection on children :

> They do not become
>> Mad
> For their parents.

---

[1] *Senryū : Japanese Satirical Verses*, by R. H. Blyth, Hokuseido Press, Tokyo, 1949.

The frontier between *senryū* and *haiku* is sometimes difficult
to locate :

> At a single match
> The darkness
> Flinches.

And if the following is not a *haiku* then it must only be
because the participants in the *Bon odori*, the dances during the
Buddhist Festival of All Souls, refrain from any elevated
sentiments concerning the impermanence of human life :

> Throwing them up to the moon,—
> Throwing them down on the grass,—
> The hands of the dancers.

I find the next *senryū*, of the student communicating with his
dead parents who perhaps endured hardship to send him to
the university, more moving than any *haiku* I have come
across. It is ' contemporary ' enough :

> Making known
> At the Buddhist family altar,
> That he has received a doctorate.

Senryū are not mentioned in the English histories of Japanese literature, and the Japanese themselves tend to look down
on them. There are no doubt good literary reasons for
this—it is true that *senryū* have something of the character
of newspaper ' fillers '—but I should be loath to believe that
it was solely due to their lack of ambiguity, subtlety or
profundity; or that *senryū* are not taken seriously on the
grounds that they are merely about human beings in their
less exalted moments. Conflagrations are still only too
common in Japan; the Japanese faced this continual danger
with a poetical image, ' *Yedo no hana* ' (' the flowers of
Tokyo '); and the *senryū* adds, in the true spirit of the
' poor man's *haiku* ' :

> ' My wardrobe
> Was about here ';
> Scratching in the ashes.

At the end of his *History of Japanese Literature*, published in 1899, W. G. Aston stated, ' The day of Tanka and Haikai seems to have passed. These miniature forms of poetry are now the exception and not the rule.' In the fifty-five years since then the country has experienced unique vicissitudes, physical and moral. The novel has plumbed the very depths of what we cynically call ' Psychology '. Yet a reasonably busy colleague tells me that he averages three hundred *tanka* per year and a number of them are printed in one or other of the magazines devoted to the craft. And the publisher of the magazine *Haiku Kenkyū* (' *Haiku* Research '—the word ' *kenkyū* ' I have found impossible to elude for long in Japan) estimates the number of Japanese *haiku* poets currently at ' easily four million '.

Let those Europeans who have grown *blasé* about ' modernism ' come and live in Japan (I mean the living Japan) for a while ; it will soon cure them of their sophisticated nostalgia for ' the past ', in whatever aspect. Among western intellectuals the word ' progress ' has become a kind of bad joke— here they could refresh their memories of what ' feudalism ' means in personal relations and what a closed system means in art and thought.

To reproach the Japanese for the thinness of their poetry would be no fairer or more useful than scolding the English for their weak performance in, say, ceramic art and sculpture. The foregoing remarks have been provoked solely by that curious ' mystique ', that aura of sanctity, which has come to surround the *tanka* and *haiku* : the insufficiently concealed feeling that the little is *per se* superior to the big, and that, since moments of perception can only be brief and unasked-for, there is no call for the poet to labour unduly over his verses. I am committing a very un-Japanese act, and sticking my neck out, but—it seems to me that the confusion between religion (Buddhism, that is) and various forms of art (poetry, painting, tea-ceremony, flower-arrangement and landscape-gardening, for instance) has led to the obscuration of the

first and the enfeeblement of the second. (The phrase in
which the author of the celebrated *Book of Tea* described
the tea-ceremony—' a religion of the art of life '—is worth
a little study.)   As Mr. Blyth implies, the poem does not
begin with a capital letter or end with a full stop.   Like tea-
ceremony and even blossom-viewing and moon-viewing, it
peters out in a vague wave of the hand towards a God who
doesn't seem to be there.   ' Where man is not, nature is
barren '—and God, too, grows distressingly indistinct.

Men and women do perforce exist, though severely cir-
cumscribed, in the Japanese theatre.   And I think it is there
that, so far, the nation's artistic strength has lain.   Their
drama owes nothing to the Chinese theatre, which it far
surpasses.   To some extent its development runs parallel to
that of the English drama : *Nō—Bunraku—Kabuki*, instead
of Miracle and Morality plays—Interludes—the great Secular
Drama.   But the comparison should not be carried too far,
since *Kabuki*, though far less religious than *Nō*, contains
considerably more explicit ' morality ' than the plays of
Shakespeare.[1]

It is heretical to express a preference for *Kabuki* over the
older and aristocratic form of *Nō*.   Of old, while *Nō* players
were treated with the utmost respect, *Kabuki* actors were outcasts, counted with the numerals used to count animals.
Today even *Kabuki* is in some degree time-honoured and
' high-brow ', but to the Japanese connoisseur of *Nō* it remains the ' popular theatre ' as which it began.   A cut above
Takarazuka Girls' Opera, admittedly, but all the same vulgar,
lacking in ' literary ' interest and tending towards amusement.
One recent foreign historian defines it as ' a modernized,
expanded, and rather debased form of the *Nō* '.   Again, the
irritating thing about *Nō* is the amount of ' cult ' which has
accumulated about it : it is religious, it is remote, and its
texts are immensely difficult to follow with much assurance.

[1] ' The drama became a storehouse of history, and a great moral
force for the whole social order of the Samurai.'   ' Fenollosa on
the Noh ', *The Translations of Ezra Pound*, London, 1953.

It is not merely that *Nō* is a religious art, but that it is art-cum-religion, a mixture which always fills me with misgivings. This highly ambiguous sentence of Yone Noguchi, regarding ' appreciation ', indicates how esoteric the *Nō* cult has become : ' When we must spend two or three years in realizing how many others fail in becoming *Nō* appreciators, it means that those elected in this particular art, where appreciation is not less, perhaps is greater, than the acting itself, will find their own lives vitalized with the sense of power in Japanese weariness.'

The subject matter of *Nō* is invariably gloomy in its Buddhist way (though once again a certain ' relaxation ' is secured by interspersing farces, *kyōgen* or ' mad words ', which sometimes parody the serious plays) ; the costumes are magnificent ; and the dancing consists of an even sequence of poses, so that the slow lifting of a fan by several inches may indicate an ecstasy of joy or of sorrow. The acting is subject to strict conventions, and Ezra Pound must have been intoxicated by his love for ' Tradition '—or perhaps his hatred for ' our theatre . . . where the paint must be put on with a broom '—when he remarked approvingly that *Nō* was ' a stage . . . where the poet may even be silent while the gestures consecrated by four centuries of usage show meaning '. I am in no position to take up the cudgels against the scholars—but I cannot help wondering whether this preference for *Nō* is not connected with the Japanese *penchant* for the disciplined and the difficult and their suspicion of the energetic and the comparatively humane ?

Of the energy of *Kabuki* there can be no doubt ; and I cannot imagine that the most austere foreigner would be aware of its ' vulgarity '. The bridge through the auditorium—*hanamichi*, ' Way of Flowers '—is reminiscent of the Elizabethan stage ; the tension in the audience as the actors enter along it or leave, passing at head-level, has to be experienced to be believed. The exit of the actor Ichikawa Ennosuke, as Benkei, at the end of the famous *Kanjinchō* was certainly one of the most impressive things, at the same time richly comic and full of power, that I have seen on any stage. Movement in *Kabuki* is certainly not ' realistic '—the actors all along have based their gestures on the rhythms of the puppets—but it is that right kind of stylization which has not lost touch with its human origins. The modern *Kabuki* theatre makes use of the most ingenious stage devices, the scenery is frequently elaborate, and the costumes are gorgeous. But the very heart of it is the actor. The actors of the first grade are revered figures, who live for their art and make considerably less money out of it than does the average radio singer. Their ambition is to die on the stage, and they never talk of retirement, though the physical exertion involved— quite apart from the vigorous oratory—exceeds that generally demanded of the ballet dancer. An important feature of true *Kabuki* is that women's parts are taken by men, specialists known as *onnagata*. A *Kabuki* actor recently explained the failure of attempts to introduce women actors on the grounds that a woman was ' too real '. And yet the fact that the extreme stylization of the acting still contrives to express nature is borne out by the impossibility one sometimes finds of persuading foreign visitors that they have not been watching a very gifted actress. It might be added that there is not the slightest unpleasantness about the performance of *onnagata* —which is more than one can say for the Takarazuka Girls as they impersonate gay cavalry officers from Old Vienna.

Kanjinchō, like all the most famous *Kabuki* plays, is a historical piece, and its theme is that of loyalty to a master. These *jidai-mono*—which were banned during the Occupation—have been likened by foreign admirers to the history plays of Shakespeare. In point of pageantry there is a similarity; but where character creation is concerned even Richard Crookback would be too subtle a figure for the *Kabuki* stage. It is easy to believe that the literary value of *Kabuki* plays, in isolation, is small, and that their emotional range is narrow. Their situations run to form—a conflict of loyalties (though the correct choice is bound to have been already prescribed by custom), an inappropriate affair of the heart (which, again, can only end in one way), or the duty of avenging oneself, one's family or one's lord. (One can see why Mr. Morris during the Occupation was of the opinion that ' it might even be desirable to close the theatre altogether for the time being ' ; the question is whether banning ever accomplishes anything other than increasing the public taste for what is banned.) It is not novelty of situation that the audience expects, nor complicated emotions, nor real problems of responsibility. And yet their behaviour is akin to that which we associate with the playgoers of Shakespeare's time—a lively mixture of immense enthusiasm and disrespectful participation, of belly laughs and truly audible sobs ; and they receive their favourites with the kind of acclamation which one had feared was now the monopoly of baseball players and professional wrestlers. In the play's duller moments they will turn their backs to it and converse gently or dig through their little tins of dried fish and rice and pickles. A visitor from a country where even the most senseless and trivial play is received in dead silence will find this sudden rising and falling of audience tension, this oscillation between yelling and sobbing and chewing and drinking, rather odd to begin with. But it is also eminently practical in that a *Kabuki* programme lasts for six hours and a number of the spectators will attend two such programmes in the same day. G. S. Fraser remarks ' how much the Kabuki play is a family pleasure—one feels it represents for the typical Japanese family what we call in England a " treat " '.[1] Certainly the atmosphere of the theatre is one which personally I much prefer to the hushed silence of *Nō*, where the audience are engrossed in following the text in books.

But though *Kabuki* has many of the characteristics of a ' popular drama ', and every performance I have witnessed has enjoyed a full house, it has to be admitted that no serious threat is offered to cinema box-offices. Our maid roared with laughter whenever we announced we were going to *Kabuki* and advised us earnestly to go to the Girls' Opera

[1] *Impressions of Japan, and Other Essays*, Tokyo, 1953.

instead. Nonetheless there are seven specifically *Kabuki* theatres—three in Tokyo, two in Osaka, one in Kyoto and in Nagoya—and their patrons are more truly a cross-section of the population than are those of the Shakespeare Memorial Theatre or the Old Vic.

For the modern playwright who wishes to express the spirit of his own time, *Kabuki* traditions clearly have little help to offer. As for the *Shingeki*, the ' New Drama '— Ibsen, Tchekhov, Hauptmann and Shaw are nothing new in Japan. The young dramatist is faced with the problem of finding a middle way between the Old and stylized and the New and realistic. In that respect his problem does not differ from that facing our English theatre ; and we must hope that he will find a workable solution more quickly than we have.

To complain that traditional Japanese poetry seems arty and insubstantial in comparison with western poetry is not very relevant. I do not wish to associate myself with the gentleman who wrote in *Time*, under the heading GULLIVER IN KIMONO, about Akutagawa's *Kappa*, ' To American Readers, Ryunosuke Akutagawa's satire seemed almost too good to have been written by a Japanese.' Nor can I much admire the Japanese publisher who printed this recommendation on the wrapper of the English translation of that clever and disturbing little novel. My point is that this poetry seems curiously bloodless and academic by the side of Japanese *Kabuki* and *Ukiyo-e* (more particularly, the work of Hokusai). It is ironical to note that the western enthusiasm for *Ukiyo-e* prints was at first (perhaps still is ?) considered by Japanese connoisseurs as a sign of vulgarity and of absence of spirituality. They prized far more highly the aristocratic, sequestered and vaguely ' symbolic ' nature painters, just as they preferred the aristocratic *Nō* to the popular *Kabuki*.[1] The

[1] Cf. Kakuzō Okakura, *The Ideals of the East* (London, 1903) : ' The Popular School . . . though it attained skill in colour and drawing, lacks that ideality which is the basis of Japanese art . . . Great art is that before which we long to die.'

popular colour prints were used as wrapping paper until Edmond de Goncourt and other French amateurs wrote them up. Now the rarer prints fetch remarkably high prices from foreign and native bidders, and the tourist will find no bargains in the little shops of Kyoto.

Perhaps signs of this derogatory attitude can be seen in the very names : *Kabuki* comes from an old word meaning ' to lose one's balance.' or ' to be playful ', while *Ukiyo-e* means ' pictures of this floating world ' or, as my dictionary has it, ' this fleeting or miserable world, so full of vicissitudes and unsettled '—that is to say, it treated of people of the middle and lower classes, at work, at play, eating, sleeping, enjoying themselves in the public baths, or searching for fleas. Westerners who think of Hokusai as an arrant caricaturist or a searcher after the curious need only step into a suburban train on a summer's evening. There, clogs dropped, squatting on the seat, his *yukata* pulled up above plump hairless thighs and the contours of a magnificent pot-belly clearly revealed, will surely be at least one figure straight out of Hokusai.

The identification of ' serious ' art with the ' aristocratic ' persists obstinately in Japan, even though the mass of the people (including the intellectuals) are living in genteel poverty or worse. And the strange thing is that it persists in the absence of any social snobbery which might otherwise encourage it. No Japanese man of taste is going to decry *Ukiyo-e* openly after it has won so much fame abroad ; similarly the film critics here were ready to reconsider their views of *Rashōmon* and *Jigokumon* when those films gained international awards.[1] And we had better point out, before we

[1] But perhaps they were right after all, from their own point of view. Better for Japan would be some competent and thoughtful films set in contemporary society (I am not thinking of atom bomb shockers or complaints about life near military bases : Japan is bigger than both of those). But costume pieces like *Rashōmon*, *Jigokumon* and *Ugetsu Monogatari* are the ones to win prestige abroad. A recent film, *Seven Samurai*, though historical, does give

forget, that whatever generalizations we make about ' Japanese cultured opinion ', it *was* Japan that gave birth to *Ukiyo-e* and *Kabuki*.   But still there is something of the feeling that common humanity is pitch and the art that touches it is going to be defiled.   It must be confessed that the cultured Japanese could point for justification to the heaps of novels about ' low life ' which have appeared since the 1880's : ' If that is " common humanity " then I prefer cicadas, chrysanthemums and my ancient pond . . .'

We find *Ukiyo-e* prints on the walls of foreigners' houses. In the better Japanese houses you will see Zen-sodden *kake-mono*, scrolls, in many of which evocativeness is carried as far as it will go.   Some of the most prized, indeed, are simply calligraphy—prized, not for the sentiment expressed but for the ' significant form ' of the brush strokes.

Well, good calligraphy is much to be preferred to incompetent representation or sentimental ' human interest '. But . . .

an intimate and unromanticized picture of peasant life in feudal times—the drawback for foreign audiences is the length of the film and the time it takes to get started.   Toshirō Mifune, the bandit of *Rashōmon*, gives a superb comic performance at times reminiscent of *Kabuki*.

TEA CEREMONY

The garden is not a garden, it is an
     expression of Zen;
The trees are not rooted in earth, then:
     they are rooted in Zen.
And this Tea has nothing to do with thirst:
It says the unsayable. And this bowl
     is no vessel: it is the First
And the Last, it is the Whole.

Beyond the bamboo fence are life-size people,
Rooted in precious little, without benefit of
     philosophy,
Who grow the rice, who deliver the goods, who
Sometimes bear the unbearable. They too
     drink tea, without much ceremony.

So pour the small beer, Sumichan. And girls,
     permit yourselves a hiccup, the thunder
Of humanity. The helpless alley is held by
     sleeping beggars under
Their stirring beards, and the raw fish curls
At the end of the day, and the hot streets cry
     for the careless scavengers.

We too have our precedents. Like those who
     invented this ceremony,
We drink to keep awake. What matter
If we find ourselves beyond the pale,
     the pale bamboo?

5 : SEVEN THOUSAND TYPES OF AMBIGUITY

'Rare writings we read together and praise:
Doubtful meanings we examine together and settle'
(*T'ao Ch'ien, trans. Arthur Waley*)

THE Japanese possess a great and beneficent gift which is generally denied to the peoples of the west—a keen visual sensibility. That gift pervades the nation, it does not depend upon training, and it ranges from the delicately suggestive to the brilliant potency of *Kabuki* costumes. Within its discipline, *Kabuki* is even flamboyant, gorgeously insolent in its triumphant heroes, superbly tragic in its distressed heroines—sufficiently flamboyant to have gratified even Lord Byron. In another respect, too, the Japanese remind us of Byron: 'as soon as he reflects, he is a child'. Though famous as a race for concealing their feelings, they do not invariably show any great respect for logic—unless it happens to be accompanied by wit or poetry.

They are perhaps too easily impressed by a pun or some other happy verbal invention. An amusing comparison always allays criticism or doubt; and, though it takes time before the average student can realize that a lecturer on a serious topic like English literature might actually sink to a joke, I must confess to having taken advantage of this partiality —it covers up illogic, it turneth away wrath.

It must be granted, however, that the case of Mr. Shingorō Takaishi, who conducted a propaganda tour of America in late 1937 for the purpose of convincing the Americans that Japan was justified in fighting China, is an extreme one. 'Japan is fighting China to win her goodwill,' Mr. Takaishi told the U.S. Foreign Policy Association in New York; 'I might add that hitting someone on the head to win his good-

will is not so illogical or impossible as many of you are prone
to think. There is that old saying : " After the rain there's
sunshine." Occasional quarrels are a part of domestic tranquillity in any home. Disputes occur even among the warm-
est friends. Again, many of you, I am sure, are old enough
to remember the days of old hickory sticks used in schools.
. . .' It apparently did not occur to Mr. Takaishi that
hickory sticks are rather dissimilar from bombs and that
domestic tranquillity even in America is rarely characterized
by the periodical slaughter of one or other member of the
family. His speech does however demonstrate the truth of
what Mr. Takaishi said elsewhere during his tour : that the
Japanese were ' very poor in the art of propaganda '. Public
figures in the west have often said much what Mr. Takaishi
was saying—but they had the foresight to avoid his flood of
homely instances, his fatal Cleopatras. Had he been content
to point to Japan's rising population and its small resources
he would have propounded an honest problem which has not
yet been faced up to.

A rather more serious example occurs in Dr. Inazō Nitobe's
celebrated book, *Bushido : The Soul of Japan* (1899),[1] where
the author is telling the fictitious (*Kabuki*) story of the son of
Michizane, a noble in disgrace. The schoolmaster has been
commanded to deliver the boy's head to the father's enemy.
It is discovered, however, that a new pupil bears a close resemblance to the intended victim ; and, with his own and his
mother's approbation, he suffers decapitation as a substitute.
An officer arrives to identify and receive the head : he examines
it closely and expresses satisfaction. This officer is actually
the father of the sacrificed boy : circumstances have forced
him into service with the enemy of Michizane, his family's
benefactor. He returns home to his wife and hails her,
' Rejoice, my wife, our darling son has proved of service to
his lord ! ' Dr. Nitobe adds, ' " What an atrocious story ! "

[1] The illogic begins on the first page, in that Dr. Nitobe, exponent
of this ' Way of the Warrior ', was also a Christian from the age
of fifteen.

I hear my readers exclaim.' Not many of them did at the time—but he can count me in. However, he continues, ' This child was a conscious and willing victim : it is a story of vicarious death—as significant as, and not more revolting than, the story of Abraham's intended sacrifice of Isaac.' It had seemed to me that the significance of Abraham's intended sacrifice was that it was to a living god, not to a code of manners. And it would have been revolting, even at that, had the sacrifice been accepted. Moreover, we have no evidence to suggest that Abraham would have exhorted Sarah to rejoice.

Ambiguity interests the Japanese a good deal more than does logic, and in the pursuit thereof they exhibit an impressive ingenuity. Ambiguity is inherent in the nature of the language : where the spoken language is rich in homophones, the written language is rich in characters which convey several different meanings. A Japanese introducing himself to another Japanese will hand over his card and at the same time speak his name. Furthermore, Japanese nouns have no number, the verbs no person, and personal pronouns are generally omitted. It will be seen then that the apparently simplest seventeen-syllable poem may prove capable of widely varying interpretations, and pages of footnotes be devoted to what to us might seem a radical point—whether the poet is talking about himself, a ' you ' (singular or plural), a ' she ', a ' he ', a ' we ' or a ' they '. This laxity of structure has proved particularly fruitful to the writers of *renga* or linked verse. As an example here is an extract from the sequence *Fuyu no hi* (' Winter Days ' or, if you prefer, ' Winter Sun ') in which Bashō and four other poets participated in the year 1685. In each case, several versions are given, in ascending order of explication :

YASUI   ' My hermitage / nest-letting to the heron / in vicinity '
(the host)

        i.e. (possibly) ' My hermitage stands in such a place that I should like to let nests to herons '

        (The host lives in such a lonely spot that he desires the companionship even of wild birds)

BASHŌ   ' Hair-growing space-of-time / hidden body's situation '

i.e. ' (Her) situation is that of one who hides herself from the public gaze while (her) hair is growing '

(Bashō has taken the ' host ' of the preceding stanza as a nun. For some reason—death of husband, unhappy love affair ?—she retired to a nunnery ; now she is planning to return to the world)

JŪGO   ' Faithlessness / unbearable that milk / squeezes out, throws away '

i.e. ' Thinking of unbearable faithlessness, she squeezes out her milk and throws it from her '

(Not only has the husband or lover been false but he has also taken the baby away—as was usual in the case of divorce)

KAKEI   ' In front of not-erased memorial tablet / weeps with a heavy heart '

i.e. ' With a heavy heart she weeps before the freshly inscribed memorial tablet '

(There is no question of faithless love here ; the mother is mourning the recent death of her child)

BASHŌ   ' Shadow (subj.) / dawn coldly / fire (obj.) burning '

i.e. ' In the (same ?) winter dawn, a shadow is burning fuel ', or, to expand it, ' In the (same ?) winter dawn, a man (?) is burning fuel (in a vacant house ?), his shadow flickering (on the wall) '

(The man may be a mourner from the preceding verse : a close relative who must watch through the night, after the others have left)

In the next verse the poet drops the mourning but carries on the idea of the vacant house—' the master of which, through poverty, has abandoned it '—and this gives rise to further scenes of desolation in the succeeding verses.

In addition to this vagueness as to who is doing what to whom, further obscurity may be contributed by the modest Japanese compulsion to avoid a straightforward statement. Yone Noguchi remarked that ' vagueness is often a virtue ; a

F

god lives in a cloud; truth cannot be put on one's finger-tip ', and complained that English poets clung to exactitude ' as if a tired swimmer with a life-belt '. In *The Ideals of the East*, Kakuzō Okakura (author of *The Book of Tea*) stated that ' Not to display, but to suggest, is the secret of infinity. Perfection, like all maturity, fails to impress, because of its limitation of growth ': a theory which leaves out of account the fairly obvious fact that perfection, if one achieves it at all, is achieved only for a moment, and that there is no call to ' avoid ' it since it is only too likely to avoid you. (The extremes to which the ' mystique of suggestiveness ' has been carried is illustrated by another comment by the same writer : ' the uncovered silken end of a great masterpiece is often more replete with meaning than the painted part itself '.) Dr. Keene puts it less romantically : ' Japanese sentences are apt to trail off into thin smoke, their whole meaning tinged with doubt by the use of little particles at the end, such as " perhaps ", " may it not be so ? ".'

With the possibility in Japanese poetry of so many per-mutations and combinations of meaning it is not surprising that some Japanese scholars have carried over their native ingenuity in interpretation into their English studies. The work of William Empson and of other so-called ' New Critics ' has had an effect more clearly pernicious here than elsewhere, for it was so eminently acceptable. Certainly there is ambiguity in much English poetry ; but at the same time there is always one overwhelming significance—happily of a logical kind—which without the least derogatory intention we can call the surface meaning. Unfortunately an inevitable lack of full intimacy with English language-forms sometimes blinds the Japanese scholar to this one primary meaning—in the same way as the expert foreign scholar of Japanese verse can hardly hope to grasp all its secondary meanings without the help of Japanese commentaries—and thus distracts his attention to some very minor and probably inoperative under-meaning. Sometimes indeed to a ' meaning ' which, by the spirit of the English language, simply cannot exist. It occasionally proves very difficult to persuade him of this latter point ; he tends to see every word as existing in a void where all of its even remotely possible associations and connotations carry more or less equal weight. The manner in which English is taught in the schools—a fantastically difficult undertaking, of course—does not help the later scholar to give full importance to the context and the contextual influence of the ever present and alas indefinable ' spirit of the language '.

A study of Blake's *Songs of Innocence* has just come into my hands, in which the author discovers dark (' profound and mysterious ') meanings under the apparent light-heartedness of these fairly simple poems. He makes much of the opening of the first piece : ' Piping down the valleys wild '—' as to the preposition " down ", we are liable to skim over it without noticing any special meaning, but the writer believes that Blake has concealed in it a profound, symbolical meaning.' Something along the lines of ' down among the dead men ' is what the commentator has in mind ; but a closer intimacy with ordinary English might have caused him to stop and ask himself what word other than ' down ' the poet could possibly have used. In the best tradition the commentator throughout refuses to acknowledge the surface meaning of Blake's little songs ; thus, of the rather mawkish piece called *Infant Joy* (' " I have no name : / I am but two days old " '), he asks these two questions :

' (1) Can a new-born baby smile ? '
' (2) Is it really sweet and full of joy ? '

—like Coleridge before him, he forgets to ask whether a new-born baby can talk, let alone express itself so coyly. He continues : ' The writer, having experienced a child-birth twice, cannot but answer these questions " No ", because a baby two days old cannot see, cannot hear, much less can smile ; and it is, in fact, very ugly and looks pitiful and helpless rather than happy. In whatever way you may look at it, you will never receive such an impression as you do from the present poem.' Surely this is *sensei*-dom run mad—and one has to admit that one could match it with many examples from current English criticism of the fashionable Tremendous Trifling type. The peculiar and (I fear) characteristically Japanese slant is the insistent denigration of real things and living people : this commentator displays a lofty disdain for ' reality ' which Blake only indulged in at his most eccentric and a contempt for the human body which Blake never showed at all. Blake is, for obvious reasons, a popular research theme for the philosophically-minded : the Prophetic Books are fair game, but one is sorry to see the *Songs of Innocence* going the same way. Once again, of course, we allow for the exceptions : the *doyen* of Japanese Blake scholars, Dr. Bunshō Jugaku, remarks in his *Bibliographical Study of Blake's Note-Book* (Tokyo, 1953), that ' It was the irony of fate that Blake, who dwelt on " Minute Particulars " and hated generalization, was a constant victim of abstraction in his *Weltanschauung* '—a truth still insufficiently recognized by most English interpreters of the poet.

I hope that the foregoing criticisms will not have sounded supercilious. Considering its alien nature, it is remarkable that English should be taught so generally and up to the level which is achieved. The Japanese are said to be poor linguists, but I have noticed that if a young person is placed in an English-speaking setting where he or she is not made to feel shy it will not be long before he or she is able to speak the language with surprising adequacy. The number of students who are enabled to study in England or America is tragically small—the young man whose family can afford to send him independently is not likely to take up teaching, while the others return to teach in universities. It seems to me that it is in the high schools that the damage is done : English tends to be taught as if it were dead and some learned surgeon had already performed the post-mortem, arriving at a set of rules which is at the same time final and complicated—so complicated that the average student, rightly convinced of his inability to master the rules, is inhibited for ever from ' having a go '.

It is not only ' face ' that deters the student from trying out his English in public : it is also his terror of ' the law '. Whereas in the interpretation of literary texts the scholar is inclined to be over-ingenious in the liberties he takes, the student on the other hand tends to distrust even his common-sense when it comes to simple conversation. While I have met many Japanese school-teachers who teach English with enthusiasm and industry, I have to admit that my faith has been shaken by some of the text-books in current use. The ' quiz ' or crossword puzzle element is pronounced : the exercises might be suitable as Intelligence Tests for very young children whose mother-tongue was English—assuming of course that Intelligence is what Intelligence Tests do actually test—but for non-English-speaking boys of grammar school age they cannot fail to be stultifying. For his homework the Japanese schoolboy is presented with two columns of words and has to combine the correct male with the correct female— ' cock ' with ' hen ', ' king ' with ' queen ' and so on. In one book which I saw, the only word that could possibly be combined with ' cow ' was ' ox '. Or else he is given perfectly good sentences in the active voice and made to turn them into impossibly bad sentences in the passive voice, thus :

Question : ' They laughed at him because of what he had done.'
Answer : ' He was laughed at by them because of what had been done by him.'

And perhaps both question and answer may be just off key :

Question : ' People elected him President of the U.S.'
Answer : ' He was elected President of the U.S. by people.'

These Japanese school-teachers really do *love* the English language. It is as if they had come to the conclusion that, since for them England was physically as remote as the moon, they might as well adopt English as their own and make out of it something new. And so we have ' Japanese School English '—a highly developed language which does have points of coincidence with England's English. I can sympathize with what has happened ; I can understand the polite jealousy with which they guard their conventional usages when

they differ from ours—sometimes against Englishmen themselves, particularly against Englishmen like myself who have
to confess to never having studied English Language.   One
comes to feel that people who by dint of sheer effort and of
sheer love, and against every kind of difficulty, have made a
foreign language their own, deserve better than to be criticized
by an outsider.   After all, even if one looks at it from a
nationalistic point of view, the English language is no sensitive
plant.   I complained that English tended to be taught in the
schools as if it were a dead language—yet now I am forced to
admit that the result does have a life of its own.

But then, just as I had finished writing this, a batch of
essays arrived and put to flight all my good thoughts and
charitable feelings.   In some of these students the attitude of
' near enough is good enough ' amounts to arrogance.   Someone writes of a novelist called Haxrey and a romantic poet by
the name of Breake.   A distinguished living poet is reported
to have received his education at Harbert, Oxford and Solbom,
and afterwards to have written a suitably polyglot poem called
' Pour Quarter '.   The poet Diluice puzzled me for a while,
until I came across him again in a sentence which maintained,
in a notable sequence of near-misses, that the leading English
poets of the 1930's were ' Owen, Spencer and Diluice '.
Admittedly foreign names are bewildering—but everyone
has access to some book of reference.   But, alas, ' profundity '
—and modern poetry is notoriously a profound subject—
doesn't need to be exact.[1]

---

[1] Japanese student English hits the bull's-eye from time to time
in a quite novel and distinctively poetic way : this, for example, of
the Georgian Poets—' Before the first world war, the mild-
autumn-weather-looking appeared in the poetical world.'   It was
touching, too, to notice in a university library a copy of *A Sentimental Journey* nestling up against *G.W.R. Holiday Haunts, 1927*.
More often, though, the aptness achieved is a matter of pure
accident ; another student wrote this, of Samuel Richardson :
' By the request of publishers, he popularized his " Pamela "
designing delicate truth of little madam.'

6 : THE MAGIC OF WORDS

'If you do not know words, you cannot know men'
(Confucius)

AGAIN, the question has to be circled about : there is no easy answer. 'The Japanese' is not every Japanese : I have invented a 'Japanese teacher' who represents a non-existent mean : no doubt many teachers are more competent than him, and the rest are less competent. None of them is quite as predictable. Indeed, when we attempt to predict Japanese behaviour we may find ourselves in for a shock.

Probably every foreign teacher who comes here is taken aside by a Japanese colleague and warned thus : 'Please do not be disappointed if your students do not understand what you say. They will understand what you mean. They will *absorb* English culture from your presence.' Without understanding ? Cynically inclined though I am, I do believe there is something— though not enough—in this theory. The Japanese are frequently far more sensitive than the casual foreigner may suppose. They do 'understand by intuition' or, as their proverb has it, 'Know all of ten from hearing one'; and if this is a less reliable method than rational understanding, it is considerably quicker and occasionally serves better.

A Japanese may meet a foreigner for the first time, in company, and exchange only a few awkward words with him. Talking afterwards with that Japanese I have often been surprised by the accurate estimate of the foreigner's character and general disposition which he had formed upon such meagre evidence. The language used between unacquainted Japanese may be extremely formal and their conversation of the 'giving nothing away' variety; but on the other hand they bring into play senses other than the ear and the brain, paying more attention than we do to the tone of voice, the restrained gestures, the facial expression. Considering the rigid etiquette which in the past (at any rate) governed behaviour and prescribed utterance, there would otherwise be no way of gauging a man's individual character—the character which foreigners, with all their romancing about the ' enigmatic Japanese' and the ' Japanese Smile ', have denied to the race, and apparently much gratified the race by so doing.

The foreigner is not always aware of these more intuitive modes of comprehension, for they may not reveal themselves in the verbal response of the Japanese. It may happen that the foreigner finds the average Japanese extremely maladroit in personal contacts—asking unduly personal questions such as ' How many children have you ? ' or ' How old are you ? ' (age is a virtue here, not something to be ashamed of, so the question may be well meant), or proffering such uncalled-for information as ' I am in love with Shelley' or ' Today I am suffering in my bowels '. But the truth is that the Japanese is trying to use a mode of converse which is alien to his customs —the ' personal ' style, for he knows that foreigners are given to the ' personal touch ', using personal pronouns all the time, dropping the ' *san* ' out of sheer friendliness and kissing their womenfolk in public for the same reason—and, however *gauche* the result may seem, he makes a better showing than the above-average foreigner who attempts to meet the Japanese on their own plane of verbal contact. Moreover, it is all a desperate kind of game calculated to please the foreigner —for the Japanese will not rely on what is for him the hideously embarrassing give-and-take of question and answer for his private estimate of the foreigner.

Consequently, the foreigner who amuses himself by guying the questions or returning equivocal answers, so confident that this stupid person will never realize that he is being had— is merely showing himself up. The Japanese may not understand—but he will know what is happening ; he can quickly

sense the slightest unfriendliness or the most guarded ridicule
—and too often he will take it more seriously than it merits.
A sensitive mechanism is continually at work beneath the
impassive and sometimes seemingly witless exterior. The
Japanese woman—so I have the impression—is customarily
even more sensitive to one's unspoken thoughts and unex-
pressed feelings. And usually without seeming stupid in the
process. Possibly she does not seem stupid because she does
not care whether the foreigner thinks her so or not—her pride
has been humbled for centuries.

The Japanese lady of good class can follow a conversation
in a language of which she knows only some twenty or thirty
words with more understanding than her modesty allows her
to reveal. As for the sensitiveness of the ordinary uneducated
and comparatively unspoiled bar-girl to what is going on in
the head of a foreign customer—that is sometimes uncanny.
She will size you up before you have got yourself seated ;
she has lit a match before you have reached for your cigarettes ; when you hesitate to order another drink she appears
to know at once what is worrying you—your finances, your
head or a feeling that you ought to get back to your wife ;
she has a damp towel ready for you the moment before the
perspiration appears. Of course, male nature in bars is apt
to run to a formula ; and sometimes self-interest is involved
in her thoughtfulness. But even so the feeling of awe
which one experiences in front of such perspicacious young
women—the newcomer, that is to say, for the ' old hand ' is
tougher—is a more effective check to riotous behaviour
than any number of throwers-out. A further curb is
supplied by the sense of waste which even alcohol cannot
exorcise.

Something of this same sensitiveness is at work in ' education '. The theory that the ' atmosphere ' thrown off by a
practising poet will be especially conducive to this sort of
' understanding without understanding ' is perhaps responsible
for the Japanese custom of inviting English poets (good, bad
and indifferent) as visiting professors at their universities.

There may very well be some truth in this—the feeling of enthusiasm can be communicated, and a talent for metaphor is useful, as I have mentioned. It is the case that Japanese students are more emotional than they permit themselves to seem, and I have witnessed a whole class suddenly bowled over by a particular line from *Macbeth*. Yes, the Japanese do sometimes get a surprisingly long way without the aid of ' understanding '. But I have also too often seen a whole class desperately struggling with some fundamental misconception resulting from language ignorance to suppose that there is very much in this Japanese notion. When the time comes that Japan can afford to import more English teachers, or Britain to export them, I hope that the emphasis will be upon sensible teachers of language prepared to work hard and from scratch and without yielding too far to the gentle intimidation of their native colleagues, rather than upon ' young English poets '.

Let us concede that traditional Japanese poetry can be ' understood without understanding '—Mr. Blyth identifies the *haiku* with Zen Buddhism, and the essence of Zen, if I understand with understanding, is the achievement of understanding without the attempt to understand. But on the whole English poetry is a very different kettle of fish : in its most important parts intellectual understanding is quite as necessary as emotional response ; and intellectual understanding necessitates an embarrassing intimacy with the language.

I have suggested that the vogue which ' Empsonianism '—the hunt for extra meanings—has had here is due to the fact that it fitted in so neatly with the ancient commentator's procedure. But it may also be connected—I hope this doesn't sound too cynical—with the difficulty many Japanese encounter in the question of ' understanding '. Empson's preoccupation with ambiguities may provide consolation for the Japanese who is not too sure of the central meaning : since the full understanding of poetry, according to ' Empsonianism ', is *so* perplexed a matter, the Japanese talent for intuitive response appears to be vindicated—if the highway is so inhumanly twisted, then the short-cut comes into its own.

I have referred previously to the national weakness in logic, in intellectual persistence in carrying an argument to its end ; and Japanese themselves have said that training in clear thinking was an urgent need of the times, that it could be the only safeguard against that unquestioning loyalty which (at any rate in other people) is such a menace to peace (and such a virtue in time of war). It is not ' loyalty to the Emperor ' which is meant here, but that Japanese habit of enrolling under the banner of a political boss (as the student attaches himself to a *sensei*) and thereafter following him unquestioningly, even though it involves assassinating his opponents : the old relationship between samurai and *daimyō* in a less pretty and more dangerous guise.

Recently a university student mentioned to me that one of the lecturers had complained to his class that the Japanese people were losing their courage, for they no longer dared to defend themselves against their bad politicians. As it had not struck me that the Japanese people, as such, had shown much energy in defying their leaders in the past, I queried this remark, adding that Japan's weakness, in the past as in the present, seemed to me to lie precisely in its lack of any real public opinion forcibly expressed. 'Ah no,' the student replied, ' the teacher was not talking about public opinion— he was referring to assassination.' In the past assassination has been Japan's substitute for public opinion. Finally one man must up and kill another man : it remains a question of personalities, in itself inimical to the formation of public opinion. All that happens is that one assassination leads to another : lives, valuable and otherwise, are lost, and the situation becomes a little more obscure and irrational than it was before.[1] Something of the same cast of mind—what we might term, in as unsensational a manner as possible, the ' assassination mentality '—lingers on among the intelligentsia. A few months ago a Japanese writer expatiating in the Japanese

[1] See newspaper cutting on p. 197.

press on that perennial topic, the iniquities of Shigeru Yoshida, the Prime Minister, suddenly dragged in the person of the Prime Minister's son, Kenichi Yoshida, a scholar and man of letters. We all love Kenichi, said the writer, we all think he's a fine fellow. But this attitude of ours is all wrong. What we should do is get together and agree to ostracize him. In this way we should register our protest against his wicked father and bring pressure to bear on him. All this was said in dead earnest. If the intelligentsia should ostracize Kenichi Yoshida, it would certainly be their loss; he is one who genuinely understands Europe and its culture and yet has remained discernibly Japanese, and he is also a notable exception to the rule of gloom among intellectuals.

I do not mean to suggest that logic can ever be a substitute for *kokoro*—that strange Japanese word, which means mind, spirit, heart, sentiment, affection and courage at the same time. But I have in mind the difficulty experienced by foreigners asked to put into decent English some article written by a Japanese. Let us suppose that it is an article on the atom or hydrogen bomb from the pen of a famous scientist : the writer is so indignant, excited and distressed, so full of *kokoro* of various kinds, that the poor translator is forced to re-write the article and say what he supposes the scientist would have meant had he not renounced meaning. This emotionality is particularly ominous under the present circumstances—it explodes on the extreme Right and it explodes on the extreme Left, while those sensible and feeling Japanese of the middle way are left looking very drab. They may have honest bread to offer, but the others control the circuses.

' Suggestiveness ' may be a good thing in poetry—as long as there is a backbone of certitude—but in politics it is wholly bad. Perhaps in *haiku* it does not matter terribly that one cannot be sure of precisely who is feeling precisely what (personally I like to know), but in a political manifesto one ought to be able to get some kind of hold on the underlying principles. It is a universal phenomenon that politicians' promises belong to a class of their own—all the same, it is

nice to know what is being promised. Alas, the Japanese
language seems to be the answer to the politician's prayer.
For a Japanese friend of mine has recently published an article
whose title we might translate as 'The Magic of Words', in
which he points out the enormous potentialities of the language
for equivocation and the ensuing result that any political
speech or declaration can be interpreted by its author in different ways at different times. He is in fact bringing up to date
the old lament of the Jesuit missionary that the Japanese
language had been invented by the devil to prevent the preach-
ing of the Gospel to the Japanese. This may be why party
policy—though I must admit to knowing little about the
matter—is apt to lack those comparatively clear outlines
which it possesses in other countries. In speaking of the
Charter Oath taken by the Emperor Meiji on 6 April 1868,
'the source and foundation of Meiji policy', Sir George
Sansom remarks that 'for an important charter of this character the Oath is remarkably vague, and attempts to translate
it faithfully into English reveal that it can be interpreted in
several ways . . . domestic political strife in Japan during
the ensuing twenty years consisted largely of an argument as
to the practical intention of these various clauses'. The same
could be said of charters more recent in date.

It is interesting to study the effect on Japanese journalists
of using the English language. The majority of male Japanese (there are of course individual protestants) accept geisha
as a part of the landscape : it is taken for granted that business
men should patronize them, and their position remains roughly
what it has been for two centuries. But when a newspaper
man 'takes up' the matter in an English-language journal he
investigates it under a western aspect : we hear of the 'soul'
of the geisha in question, the writer refers to 'this wicked
world', he quotes from the English poets, he remarks that
the notables concerned in the ship-building scandals were an
instance of 'gilded honour shamefully misplaced', he comes
out with the accurate statement that a geisha's virginity is
sold for so much money—'a case of "maidenly virtue

rudely strumpeted " '. It has to be allowed that his article
' trails off into thin smoke ' at the end :

> Altogether, Geisha is a unique existence, beautiful but pathetic.
> . . . Its usefulness cannot be denied but in spite of its colour and
> charm, we must remember that Geisha is not a woman half so gay
> as the lively tune of the ' Amorous Goldfish '—of Sydney Jones'
> operetta ' Geisha '—would have us imagine.

Indeed not. Even so, my point is that using English has
forced this journalist to make statements which are more
definite than they might have been otherwise. There are
not so many opportunities for euphemism in English as in
Japanese. (And the geisha world is especially rich in poetic
euphemism : one reason why, perhaps, it has successfully
dazzled so far the weak eyes of public opinion.) English
does call a spade a spade more frequently than does Japanese ;
it is, if you like, a more ' humanistic ' language in that its
tendency is always to draw the attention of the user to the
human realities of the subject in hand. Even its poetry—to
judge from the examples with which the journalist fortified
himself—puts things not unplainly.

As the reader will have gathered by now, I am not one of
those well-meaning foreigners who, after a horrified glance at
the jazz records piled up in the chromium-plated little shops,
and the glassy little cabarets and the Frenchified little cafés,
sternly advise the Japanese to return post-haste to their Old
Traditions. I should rather exhort them to commit *hara-kiri*
—one of these old traditions. ' East is East and West is
West ' is a comforting apophthegm, but it is no longer true,
for good or bad. It is too late in the day for us to go back ;
we have to endure the inartistic horrors of the way forward.
What is essentially ' Japanese ' about the Japanese will survive
without the solicitous help of foreigners, and the rest can be
spared. Do we want to tie them up in some kind of ' Indian
Reservation ' where they can get on with the worship of
Amaterasu *et sequitur* and the manufacture of fans and dolls
for export ? We ought to remember that if we managed to
do so—which in any case is out of the question—we should

also be condemning them to the tyranny of some sort of 'samurai code' and probably cheapening the already low price of women on the open market.

But the foregoing outburst needs to be apologized for : it really belongs to another chapter. The point I really wanted to make was that a training in the use of English (French would do equally well, but English happens to have the start of it) might be of use to the Japanese as they move into their new life—into that world which in the end will be either One World or No World at all. This is no high-flown dream of mine : I am not suggesting that the English language offers a panacea for all the diseases of mankind. Obviously a fool is a fool and a criminal a criminal whatever language he speaks. But for Japan to live in peace the first domestic necessity is the all-round improvement of social conditions, and that work will have to be carried out with deliberation and without excitement. And the English language does offer a discipline in avoiding the extremes (one that could be useful to the future Japan in more ways than our traditional 'discipline', Latin, was to us) ; it is a language of moderation and of the concrete, and it is not over-rich in euphemism or other modes of evasion, whereas experience leads me to believe that the Japanese language tends to act either as rose-coloured spectacles or else as mud-coloured ones. It is too prone to show itself either over-delicate, abstract and non-committal—as in the poets—or else, as in much contemporary journalism, bloodily sensational and inclined to hysteria.

Of course English will have to be taught soundly ; and, if I may say so, in a reasonably English way. Nor should its study on this level be confined to future business men and foreign office officials. It is those men whose influence, in the long run, is wider whom I have in mind. I see that I have returned to my old plea for more interchange of teachers between our two countries.

And now, for the sake of a little and not irrelevant light relief, let us look at some recent examples of what Basil Hall

Chamberlain called ' English as she is Japped '.[1] Public English of this species is no longer as riotously funny as it was when Professor Chamberlain collated such specimens as ' Extract of Fowl ' (over an egg shop) or

' JAPAN INSTED OF COFFEE (i.e. *Japanese substitute for coffee*) : More men is not got dropsg of the legs who us this coffee, which is contain nourish '

or (a hotel notice in Kyoto),

' NOTICE TO THE DEALERS.

On the dinning-time nobody shall be enter to the dinning-room, and drowing-room without the guests' allow. Any dealer shall be honestly his trade, of course the sold one shall be prepare to make up the safe package '

These days the tradesmen are more wary about clothing Japanese idioms in English words. After all, the sign which hangs under Sannomiya railway arches (not the most refined area of Kobe)—' COME COME BABY—ENGLISH CONVERSATION SCHOOL '—probably did proclaim quite accurately the aims of an Occupation-inspired institution. On the whole there is an honest attempt to achieve the ' spirit of the language ', and it does not behove us to put on superior airs. Had history impelled English shop-keepers, hotel-managers, publicans and students to conjure with Chinese characters . . .

The old HEAD CUTTER has disappeared ; the profession has unanimously adopted the more enticing designation BAR BER, from which nothing will budge them—presumably on the analogy of the swarming hordes of BAR this and BAR that. BAR LIFE (i.e. ' bā raifu ') we had to re-christen BAR DEATH after the night when we found it full of unconscious bodies, a ' hostess ' being sick into the palmetto and the tough little madame unconcernedly counting the takings. BAR DOM truly seemed afflicted with boredom, while BAR MONTPALNAS demonstrates the all-pervading confusion between ' l ' and ' r '. The former sound does not exist in Japanese and ' r '

[1] *Things Japanese*, London, 1890.

takes its place, as in ' Rondon '. Radio programmes printed in the English-language papers are especially prone to this error of identity ; for example, ' Pereas and Mersande ' and the English composer, ' Parser '. But the classical instance is that mentioned by Sherard Vines in 1931, a large poster hanging over a Tokyo station : ' SUNLIGHT SOAP. LEVER BROTHELS LIMITED.' [1] Then there are the bars with arty names, such as BAR MARIE LAURENCIN, BAR RENOIR, BAR KISSLING [sic] and BAR RIMBAUD. The girls in BAR RIMBAUD did know that their patron saint was a French writer of some kind ; but in these cases the artiness goes no further than the door. When nomenclature is concerned, ' things French ' are definitely predominant. ' Pascal ', happily, is a respectable coffee-shop in Kobe. A district in Tokyo is known as ' French Alley ' because of its many coffee-shops and bars with such names as ' La Vie en Rose ', ' Avec ', ' Moulin Rouge ' and ' Sous les Toits de Tokyo '. The modishness of existentialism is demonstrated by the foolhardy name of another Tokyo bar— ' La Peste '.

But Beer Halls, a pre-war importation from Germany, are becoming increasingly popular, especially among those who want to drink and not to dally. The legend ALASKA BEAR HALL is slightly annoying, as it is flashed several times daily on the screen of the Asahi cinema, and the two are auxiliaries of the *Asahi Shimbun* (the leading Japanese daily, which also runs a very creditable evening paper in English). This may be another instance of Japanese vulnerability to suggestion :

[1] Rather similar is the Middle-Eastern confusion between ' p ' and ' b '— an Egyptian student of mine once achieved the glorious slogan, ' this Age of Atomic Pomp '. It is interesting to compare the ' un-Englishisms ' of Japanese and Egyptian students. My experience has been that those of the Egyptians are predominantly comic in spirit—slovenly, a bit brutish, cavalier, unpredictable but yielding to elucidation, orotund and occasionally superb. Those of the Japanese, on the other hand, are predominantly tragic—contorted, agonized, tight-lipped, sometimes baffling, consistent and insistent, and occasionally poetic in a gently sad sort of way.

the trade-mark of the ' BEAR HALL ' is actually a polar bear
(Alaska-air-conditioning-iced-beer) who appears in the publicity looking suitably proud of himself. The least pre-
tentious type of small bar is often called a BEER STAND, or
sometimes STAND BAR : I have heard of one describing itself
as STAND BARE, though I have not actually seen it.

Truly speaking, Japanese is not a language, but a set of
languages ranging from the rather exquisite formality of a
cultivated public speaker to the racy speech of the streets.
On its lower levels, at any rate, it is a very receptive language.
It is always ready to take words and idioms from abroad and
to assimilate them in such a way that they re-emerge in no time
looking—at least to a novice—remarkably Japanesey. A
study of these foreign terms is both amusing and instructive
in casting light on East–West relations and on the current
Japanese sociology. It deserves a book to itself, though the
writer would have to be that rare bird, a scholar with popular
contacts.

In the hopes that they may tempt such a scholar, I append
a few of the commoner examples. With circumstances
changing so rapidly ever since Japan was opened to the west,
many of these expressions have had but a short life. A
Japanese friend remarks humorously that ' haikara ' has
passed out of the colloquial tongue into the classical language :
deriving from ' high collar ' some forty years ago, it originally
signified a fashionable importation from the west, either
manners or material, the latest thing in smartness. Later on,
partly perhaps because of the shocked reactions of foreigners
but chiefly owing to the rise of nationalism and a return to
' things Japanese ', it came to have the derogatory significance
of crude and vulgar imitation of things foreign (for example,
the so-called ' foreign-style house '). These days the term
has disappeared altogether—one is glad to get whatever one
can afford, to eat or to live in, whether traditional or modern,
high-collar, low-collar or open-neck.

' Modan boi ' and ' modan gărŭ ' also originated in the

world of post-First-World-War and are now out of date. Typical treatment was accorded to these terms in that, having been received into the spoken language, they were speedily abbreviated. (The Japanese language is agglutinative, but the Japanese have a genius for abbreviation which the Germans would do well to study.) Thus the male became ' mobo ' (a tastier designation than our ' spiv ') and the female ' moga '. ' Modan gărŭ ' was already derogatory from its beginnings ; it was rather worse than ' flapper ' and had no connotation of ' advanced thought ' about it—for the ' New Woman ', I am glad to say, a reasonably neutral Japanese word was used (*seitōha* : ' blue stocking school ')—and a witty professor of Waseda University found Chinese characters which produced the sound of ' modan gārŭ ' and the meaning of ' hair-cutting frog '. That is to suggest, ' a girl whose bobbed hair makes her look like that base, empty-headed and ever-chattering creature, the frog '. But the Waste Land of post-Second-World-War Japan required something even more derogatory than ' moga '. The French expression ' après-guerre ' was a gift for Japanization—it became ' apŭre ' and then, by a natural transition, the expression ' apŭre gārŭ ' (' post-war girl ') came into being. The Japanese tongue is deficient in terms of abuse, but it can make a foreign expression sound very nasty. ' Onna-boi ' for a person of indeterminate sex is another instance of this—though otherwise it is a pleasing mixture of tongues, since *onna* is the standard Japanese word for ' woman '. Happy to say, in business, science and the teaching of literature, we *have* supplied a few respectable terms.

' Pan ' (bread) is one of the few Gallicisms which came to stay. ' Shappo ' was an early usage, but the course of history has more recently supplanted it with ' hatto '. A current sophisticated colloquialism of French derivation is ' abbekkŭ ', used in the sense of ' going out with ' a member of the opposite sex. Its significance may be darker, as this back-translation in the English-language press indicates : ' Economic necessity has forced many Japanese girls into prostitution or " avecing ".'

The 'courting' seats in cinemas are known as 'avec seats', moreover, just as the little double seats in the coaches of one of the electric railways running between Osaka and Kyoto are called 'romansŭ shīto'. A term of similar social status is 'ōnri': the Japanese girl suffering from 'economic necessity' who is lucky enough to 'go steady' with a G.I. refers to him as 'watakŭshi no ōnri'—'my only'.

German has contributed that sombre word 'arŭbaito', used exclusively of the work whereby a student supports himself (or herself—see 'arbeit salon', later). And another grim Germanism is 'rumpen', vagabond, from *Lump* (ragamuffin or good-for-nothing).

'Ōbākōtō'—which doesn't need translating if one remembers that 'b' stands in for 'v'—is another convincingly 'Japanese' word: it too has experienced the linguistic shears and is more common in the form 'ōbā'. 'Sābisŭ' means 'service', but in the restricted sense of something provided free of charge. And the gluey hair-oil with which the Japanese subdue their obstinate hair is called 'chikkŭ', from the Japanese pronunciation of 'cosmetic'.

Naturally many expressions pertaining to sports and to politics (two rather new and rather popular institutions) have been imported. Particularly those connected with labour disputes, themselves a recent importation: 'strike' was first Japanized as 'sŭtoraiki' and then shortened to the expressive 'sŭto' (the 'u' is practically elided, producing an explosive sound), while 'General Strike' is a little less obvious under the guise of 'zenesŭto'. 'Demonstration' (i.e. political) was adopted as 'demonsŭtoreisyon' and then adapted to—what suggestion do we have here?—'demo'. 'Sabo' is a particularly interesting coinage (which is now used in regular grammatical form): coming from 'sabotage', it is employed of absenteeism in workers and of truancy or lecture-cutting in students. In the latter context it has come to have the associated meaning of 'crib', the convenient reference book which publishers thoughtfully bring out just before examination time. The student who has indulged in the first kind

of ' sabo ' during term (because of laziness or, more likely,
' arŭbaito ') has recourse to the other kind of ' sabo ' at the end
of term. ' Rasto ' is of course ' last ', used of ' the last dance '
and in other connections, such as ' rasto hebi ' (from ' last '
and ' heavy '), a term employed in athletics to signify the last
effort or the final spurt of energy.

' Apāto ' and ' depāto ', though obvious enough, deserve
mention as the names of two institutions very common and
generally praiseworthy in modern Japan—apartment houses
and department stores.

And to end with, here are two examples of something rather
different, though they do demonstrate both Japanese ingenuity
in language matters and the Japanese reluctance to dispense
with the title ' san ': ' B–29 San ' (or sometimes simply
' B San ') and, a term formerly applied by Japanese girls to
padres of the Commonwealth occupation forces, ' Amen
San '. (Not to be confused with the commoner ' Ame San ',
' Mr. American ', or ' Amekō ', ' Prince ' or ' Duke American ',
as featured in the slogan ' Amekō kaere ! '—' Go home,
American dukes ! '). You may not give your cat enough to
eat, but you call him ' Mr. Cat ' all the same.

East and West do meet—though not always on altogether
happy ground—in contemporary Japanese speech.

7 : MADAM BUTTERFLY

THIS and the following two chapters have not been included for the sake of sensationalism : the phenomena which they describe do loom large in contemporary Japan. Moreover, this chapter may have a certain instructional value, in that the term ' geisha '—though the most familiar Japanese word in the outside world, except perhaps for ' kimono '—is still largely misunderstood by foreigners. Conceptions of ' the geisha girl ' range from the picture-postcard variety (a combination of Pavlova and Madame de Maintenon) to that held by the G.I.s who were reported as rolling down the Ginza yelling, ' We want geesha, we want geesha ! ' The G.I.s were certainly nearer to the truth ; the only fallacy they were guilty of lay in their lack of both an *entrée* and an expense account. No doubt their desires were attended to, in a more fitting manner.

A short historical digression might be of interest at this point. In the latter half of the eighteenth century, feudal lords had certain retainers known as ' geisha '. These were men, proficient in archery or fencing or horsemanship—the word ' geisha ' simply means a person of ' skill ' or ' attainment '. A little later (*c.* 1780) the word came to be used of women proficient in singing and dancing. Earlier the term *odoriko* had been used for the dancing girls, but as this had a secondary meaning which we might render as ' fit to be tumbled ', they naturally preferred to be known by the more neutral word. Originally there were two clearly distinguished classes of geisha : *haori* geisha and *korobi* geisha. *Haori* is a kind of coat or upper garment ; and *haori* geisha were purely musicians, that is players of *samisen* (a three-stringed guitar of plangent tone), who retailed their ' attainment ' with their coats on—in plainer terms, they did not retail their bodies. *Korobi* literally signifies 'tumbling down', which serves to denote the 'proficiency' of the second class. The *haori* geisha do still exist today : they are proud of their 'coats' and are said to dispense with *tabi* (the thick socks with a separate big toe) and to walk in their bare feet in order to show their strength of character and their independence. However, they comprise only about one per cent of the total geisha population ; and the word today is always used in the sense of 'tumbling down'.

Two cynical *senryū* indicate the true state of affairs ; this, perhaps of a vain ambition :

> Instead of her *samisen*,
> The geisha
> Took out her pillow,

and this, in which the madam displays her well-developed business sense :

> 'You couldn't live '—
> Her 'mother' told her—
> 'By your *samisen*.'

Kyoto is the heart of the geisha industry, and this chapter is based on notes taken there. The geisha world is a closed one : it has many ramifications and many ramparts, and 'investigation' by foreigners (who might turn out to be missionaries) is not welcome. The direct approach being out of the question, I was fortunate enough to be taken to perhaps the only non geisha-trade tea-house in Gion, the quarter which is the heart of the heart. This Naboth's vineyard proved a source of considerable information ; even so, a single telephone call made by the owner's wife to check on figures was sufficient to arouse suspicion.

Gion is divided into two districts—A and B. A is the superior one, and at present it consists of some four hundred geisha and thirty-five *maiko*. The *maiko*, or 'dancing girl ' as she is sometimes translated, is an apprentice geisha : she is distinguished from the geisha by two characteristics, the dangling sash (*darari*) worn around her kimono at breast-level, and her virginity.   We might conveniently begin with the *maiko*.

These girls begin their training at an early age, five or six, in dancing, singing and playing the *samisen*.   Most of Gion lives on the industry in one way or another, and the children of the area are naturally attracted to the profession, rather as English girls might be drawn, less irresistibly, towards the theatre or the cinema ; the appeal of the pretty clothes, the singing and dancing, can be imagined.   And then, of course, daughters may be sold into the profession by their poverty-stricken parents.

The geisha house is managed by the *okāsan* (' Mother san ' as she is known to her brood—a cut above ' mamma san ') or *okamisan* (' Mrs. Upper Seat ') as the townspeople will call her.   The law forbids that anyone should trade in the flesh of another, which ultimately is what the *okāsan* is doing.   Therefore she will ' adopt ' her *maiko* and geisha—a ' mother ' can do as she wishes with her ' daughters ', and she has the blessing of the fine old tradition of filial piety.   The price paid by the *okāsan* to the original parents averages between ¥20,000 and ¥30,000 (at the present rate of exchange £20–30) ; in exceptional cases sums ranging from ¥50,000 to ¥100,000 may be handed over.   In return, the girl must serve the *okāsan* for seven or eight years.

The initial expenses of the *okāsan* are high, for she must provide her girls with clothes (a kimono and accessories cost in the neighbourhood of £100) and pay for their lessons. The complaint these days is that since the end of the war the little *maiko* is forced to attend school till the age of fifteen, thus lowering the standards of the profession.   Such is the law.   However, there are generally methods of alleviating the rigours of the law ; and it seems that the Gion schools take care not to place any undue strain on their female pupils' grey matter or to insist on regular attendance.   The treatment of *maiko* and geisha depends upon the character of the individual *okāsan*, and for her own sake she will be unlikely to misuse them.   She pays them a certain commission, *hanadai* (' flower expenses ' or, as we should say, pin money) ; if she is amiable they will be given time off to visit their families or to go to the cinema or theatre. Since they are hired out to entertain at dinner parties, they may not return home till the early hours of the morning. And since they must rest during the day, in addition to fitting in their various lessons, there may not be much time for leisure outings. However, like all Japanese women, they are adept at summing up character—the character of their *okāsan* as well as of their clients—and they know the best time to make such requests.

The *okāsan* could not keep her business going simply through hiring out her girls as skilled entertainers. Her chief source of income lies elsewhere. Every geisha must have a *dannasan*, a 'master', who possesses sole rights in her corporeal person. There is no fixed age at which a *maiko* graduates to geisha; civil law does not operate in this world. But she will take—that is, she will be given to—a *danna* at some point between fourteen and eighteen years of age, depending on the gentleman's taste. Those in touch with the profession say that they know at once when the change has taken place, by the bearing of the girl, even though she is only fourteen: she has become 'a woman'.

The *danna* is chosen by the *okāsan*, and he pays her several million yen (several thousand pounds) to acquire his rights. This payment is called *mizuage*—literally, 'water-raising'— a good example of the euphemisms current in the 'flowery world'.[1] The *danna's* rights, however, are not absolute. The geisha will still entertain for other people, at the *okāsan's* behest and to her profit; though the *danna* of course has first call on her services and she will be expected to remain faithful to him in the matter of the pillow. Nonetheless the *okāsan* sometimes intervenes to remove the *danna* and substitute a more profitable one. And the geisha may indulge in clandestine love affairs on the side—though these are best kept from the *okāsan*, unless she is a remarkably tolerant mistress.

[1] *Karyūkai* (the gay quarters) literally means 'flowery-willowy world'; the diseases which may be picked up in that world are known as *karyūbyō*, literally 'flowery-willowy sickness'.

Maiko are generally pretty, because young Japanese girls generally are pretty. Geisha—after one has recovered from the first impact of being entertained by women skilled in the relevant arts—usually turn out to be considerably less than beautiful. They are swathed in their robes : their appeal in fact is strip-tease in reverse, and it centres on the bare flesh on the base of the neck where the kimono collar sticks out stiffly at the back. To our way of feeling, the white paint used on the face is not calculated to provoke gaiety. In fact, the less one knows about geisha, the more one enjoys their presence. Their dancing is well executed, their singing likely to please even those with no ear for Japanese music, and their attentiveness is of course gratifying in the extreme. They lay themselves out to please : that is their life. Like all Japanese women engaged in dubious trades, they give the impression of devoting themselves conscientiously to an activity which they would rather have avoided had it been possible. In the end the gentle melancholy of their facial expression may cast a shadow over one's enjoyment. But that very sadness may be part of their art. Japanese men appear to like sadness in their women.

Girls born in geisha districts (there are two in Kyoto, the second being Ponto-chō) are unlikely to become legal wives in good or reasonably good families, I am told : if they marry, it will probably be into poverty. On the other hand, the standard of living in their districts is comparatively high, owing to the constant traffic with wealthy men. The girls thus grow up in what a Japanese critic of the institution described to me as ' a state of natural servility '. They have no desire to rebel against circumstances which are materially comfortable. The geisha houses are linked with the tea-houses and with the *machiai* ; [1] employment is provided for

[1] Tourists are prone to think that a geisha house is where one goes to make merry with geisha. But the geisha house is simply the living quarters of the *okāsan* and her girls. They entertain at parties held in the *chaya* (tea-house, or more accurately ' Japanese restaurant ') ; when they meet the *danna* or other gentleman client privately, it is at a *machiai*, a smaller establishment where food may

samisen makers, drum makers and kimono makers, for flute players and other musicians (who may be retired geisha) ; taxi-drivers are used to take the girls to and from parties ; local tradesmen dealing in combs and other trinkets enjoy the patronage of rich *habitués* ; and a number of professors, male and female, are kept busy imparting their knowledge. It is a compact little world. The geisha system is practically water-tight. It is not so much that there is no escape for the unwilling girl as that there is no pronounced desire to escape.

These girls, educated in the complaisant local schools, have little knowledge of the ordinary outside world : they are ' specialists ', they have an acute grasp of their clients' habits and an accumulated store of business and political secrets dropped by those clients in unguarded moments. They have little recognition of what to outsiders may seem the essential ignominy of their profession. Girls of the A district appear to be rather pleased with themselves and reasonably content with their lot. They stand a fair chance of making money and setting up later as *okāsan* themselves, or opening a bar or hotel or small restaurant. They also stand a chance of marry-ing their *dannasan*—but that is a different matter altogether.

Only a rich business man can afford the luxury of a geisha as concubine. For him, it seems, this is not so much a luxury as a necessity. And in fact the geisha-concubine is some-times described as a ' second wife ' or ' business wife '. The first wife—a lady—is naturally the pillar of his house ; and the bosom of the family is considered her rightful position. But many business deals, straight as well as crooked, are carried out in a *chaya*, and the head of the firm needs a ' busi-ness wife ' to help him there. She should possess her own set of virtues : the ability to entertain gracefully (which means anything from dancing to pouring out wine) [1] and,

be available, but which we might rather translate as ' rendezvous ' or ' place of assignation '.

[1] It may not be superfluous to add that the dancing of a geisha is the opposite of abandoned—delicate, slow and disciplined. The words of the songs are apt to be double-edged, however—but no

very important, the gift of saying naughty things in a nice way and of responding tactfully to the witticisms of a drunken guest. Most of these talents (and others besides) are possessed by the legal wife : but her presence would impose a restraint on the company which might not be good for business. A particular *chaya* may be linked with a particular firm, for entertainment purposes, just as the head of the firm may be linked with a particular geisha. It is all managed very nicely indeed.

The system of ' business wife ' is sometimes defended on moral grounds, too. A senior employee of a trading firm once told me a cautionary story. It began with a young man who had recently become head of a family business. As was the custom with that firm, arrangements were made for him to take a ' business wife '. She was young and attractive. The *mizuage* changed hands. But the young man, while agreeing to use her as his business hostess, refused to take advantage of his other rights. He argued that he was quite content with his legal wife and that she was enough for him. This was considered quite shocking. And events justified the head-wagging of his friends and relatives. For, many years afterwards, he accidentally met the woman in a train. She had finished her term as geisha and was now married, with several children. The man at once fell passionately in love with her —and disgraced himself eternally by abandoning his wife and children (the cardinal sin of betraying the family) and running away with her. ' If,' the teller wound up, ' he had been sensible in the first case, that dreadful thing would never have happened.' The man had behaved ' unexpectedly '—he had offended against the system, and the system took its revenge.

It may happen that, when a *danna's* wife dies, he will ask

knowledge of this is betrayed by the singer's expression or behaviour. Dealing in dirt, she must bear herself as if she were as pure as snow. Similarly, even the street-walkers never descend to working on their intended clients' feelings—or, perhaps, work on them by not so doing. A Japanese prostitute may obviously not be a great mind but—by the standards to which we are used—she behaves almost like a lady.

his concubine to marry him. There appears to be no social prejudice against marrying a geisha of the first class : she is a respect-worthy person, in theory at any rate she has been the mistress of only one man, and a rich man at that, which makes her an interesting person. But it is significant that such a proposition of marriage is not always welcome. More often than not the geisha prefers that her relationship with the *danna* should continue on its old basis. Paradoxically she values her independence. And so we have the odd spectacle of the more advanced type of Japanese wife pitying the geisha for her servile position, while the geisha declines the honour of entering the oppressed state of legal wifehood. She would rather look forward to her little bar, with a new generation of geisha dropping in ' for a flip word, and to tidy their hair a bit ', and the sound of *samisen* practice from the houses around her, and the big cars of clients passing through the streets, and all the gossip and the comparing of notes and the feeling of being in at the heart of momentous matters. Rather an *okāsan* than an *okŭsan* (i.e. wife—the word signifies the person in the inner or back room of the house).

But all that I have said refers only to the geisha of the A class—the queens and princesses of the profession. Those in the B class are less regal : they pass from man to man with some frequency, in fact they are ' on call ' and only their arts and graces and their comparative expensiveness save them from being described, in English at least, as prostitutes. And if they are not good at their trade—a geisha despised by her *okāsan*, who has paid good money for her, is a miserable creature indeed.

How secure is the geisha world today ? It seems to be as safe and solidly based as it ever was : and yet there is no doubt that the recent shipping scandals have drawn unfavourable attention to the flowery world. The following is an extract from a report printed in the Japanese *Weekly Asahi* :

From April until December of last year (1953), more than a hundred parties were held at the Nakagawa (tea-house) in Akasaka,

Tokyo. Among the guests were incumbent and former Cabinet ministers, other politicians and company executives. All together there were about four hundred guests and seven hundred geisha involved. Yamashita Shipping Co. alone sponsored about eighty parties at the Nakagawa and another fifty or so at the Hasegawa. The Yamashita Co. president and the managing director of the Iino Shipping Co. attended almost all the parties. . . .

Geisha usually have extremely good memories of whom they have been entertaining at parties. They can also remember well conversations they hear. If some of the Akasaka geisha would jog their memories, they would be doing their country a great service.

However, ever since the announcement of the receipt of my memorandum by the Government, business in Akasaka has fallen off. Geisha were told to retire immediately after dinner when business is being discussed. They have also been told that if they receive no calls now for some time, they will still receive compensation.

While indignation is largely directed at the politicians who so freely disposed of public funds, some of it inevitably attaches to the geisha on whom some part of these funds were spent.[1]

The likelihood of a revolt beginning within the geisha world itself seems extremely remote. Why should it? These girls are sold—but under infinitely more comfortable conditions than their poor sisters in the streets. Honest work can be found, with some effort—but ' flower money ' comes more generously. It is true that in 1937 a geisha strike broke out, involving finally three hundred girls. The geisha retreated to a Buddhist temple in the hills and refused to come down until their demands were met. Those demands were firstly for the right to select their own gentleman friends (presumably from among those able to meet the *okāsan's* fees) and secondly—rather academic—for the right to form a trade

---

[1] The phenomenon is no new one. A Japanese critic, writing before 1904, stated : ' The majority of Japanese politicians . . . are active in the fomentation of agitation, and frequent disreputable quarters to brood upon their schemes. They are addicted to dissipation and sunk in corruption.'

union. All this, however, happened in Osaka, a great modern industrial city, and it does not seem to have affected permanently the flowery world. It is significant that the article referred to on page 93 was later summarized in a Japanese digest under the title ' A Geisha in Revolt '—an oddly strong term to describe the action of the lady in question who, sick of her notoriety as the ' Scandal Geisha ', quietly disappeared from the *okāsan*'s establishment.

My ' go-between '—if I may so term that woman of both charm and independent mind—was especially interested in the possibilities of revolt within the camp. She had to admit that there were few signs of it at the moment: the only promise, indeed, being held out by a *maiko* whom we might call ' Yoshiko '. Yoshiko's mother is a successful ex-geisha, and so she is in the happy position of having her real mother as her *okāsan*. Yoshiko was ready enough to start training as a *maiko*, but when sent to one of the Gion schools she showed unexpected opposition. The standard of teaching, she announced, was low and therefore she had decided to go instead to the school attached to Dōshisha University (the famous Christian university in Kyoto). There she still is. Will she insist on going on to the university ? Will she turn out to be the Joan of Arc of Geishadom ? I can hardly think so.

It is not likely that the institution of geisha will yield before anything other than outside pressure—the pressure of public opinion. And public opinion is still in its kindergarten stage of education in Japan. The question is obviously bound up with the ' emancipation ' of women. Only when they become generally and sincerely regarded as the human equals of men, as companions as well as mothers-of-children, only when they come out of their ' back rooms ' and enter into the social life of their husbands, so that a business man will entertain *en famille* as a matter of course—only then will geisha really fall into disrepute and neglect. And that is not likely to happen soon or quickly.

The loss involved in such a radical social change may be

considerable. I am not thinking of the geisha arts, which anyway are only enjoyed by a small minority,[1] but rather of the possible loss of the graces of ordinary femininity (with apologies to Dr. Summerskill). Enough has been written about the charm of the better-class Japanese wife—her gracefulness, her considerateness, her courtesy towards others, her exquisite taste in clothes—and much of it is true. Her superiority over the Japanese male in these respects may be connected with her official inferiority to him : having been cut off from so much of life, she has had time to develop to an unparalleled extent the talents and activities proper to the person 'within the house'. Like the geisha, she too is a product of specialization. Within the limits of her experience, she makes her social equivalent in the west look insensitive, hoydenish and unsexed—but I have known members of her class who were unable to cross a busy street by themselves.

But the movements of the world cannot be halted, they can only be guided. I suspect that in many families today the subservient attitude of the wife is only kept up because it is the 'expected' thing and that neither the man nor the woman really wants it. Among many young couples, both partners perhaps university graduates, the pretence is no longer kept up. I have it on the best authority that nowadays more and more Japanese husbands are helping to wash the dishes and clean the house. They exclaim a little ruefully, 'Well, this is what democracy means!', but they do it all the same. These young housewives may prove one of 'democracy's' mainstays, if the test should come.

[1] Except, that is, for the yearly dances performed publicly by the geisha of Gion and Ponto-chō in their own theatres : these are very popular both with ordinary Japanese and with foreigners. Here, too, the illusion is of a highly disciplined doll : the training is towards removing the girl from a state of humanity to the condition of a minor work of art. The charm is undeniable. The only false note proceeds from the thought that these little works of art are handed over to a *danna* for all-too-human usage on payment of a substantial sum of material banknotes.

5. Gion *maiko*.

6. Ponto-chō: the narrow alley, running parallel to the Kamo River, one of the two geisha quarters of Kyoto.

The geisha world is a large structure, embellished with considerable external elegance and taste. That it is founded on the sale of human beings and the denial of elementary human rights, however, is certain. That Japanese woman-hood may lose in sweetness and grace through its eventual decay is only a supposition. The reformers are in the right —even those Japanese husbands who hardly seem to recognize the implications for themselves of the reforms they desire—and, Japan being what she is, reform will be a slow process, slow enough to enable whatever good elements depend upon the wife-geisha antithesis to survive the downfall of the system.

But I must confess to a lack of the missionary spirit where geisha are concerned. 'Liberty' in the abstract is not a banner I am especially impelled to fight under. There are worthier objects of one's concern—people who do less well out of selling themselves. If social conditions can be improved in general—if living space and working space can be found for the common and multitudinous people of this land, and a less capricious security provided against illness, accident and old age—then the little camp of geisha will gradually crumble away. And then visitors from abroad will have one more reason for lamenting over the awful western-ization of Japan. What, no geisha girls ? [1]

[1] The idea that geisha are cultivated in the arts (i.e. outside their own) is probably connected with the pre-war custom among writers of meeting in *chaya* and *machiai*. The spirit of the *salon* is still remote from the Japanese : writers were so formal, stiff and cautious that it was hardly possible for them to exchange views (for example, to take part in one of those intellectual symposia which are rather popular here) without the presence of *sake* and geisha. It is the same today, in that a modicum of alcohol works wonders in loosening the cagey intellectual tongue and relaxing the stiff artistic neck—though writers have had to yield up the *machiai* and the geisha to business men and politicians, and meet instead in modest restaurants or bars.

H

8 : AND MISS MOTH

THIS will be a very short chapter.   But it would be an offence against Japanese thinking to muddle in *jorō* and *pan-pan* with geisha ; and something more emphatic than a new paragraph must separate them.

For the *jorō* rank below the lowest grade of geisha.   They are the prostitutes who live in the brothels of the licensed quarters ; and they are endowed with little of the romantic aura which surrounds Madam Butterfly.   They too are sold by their parents—to the mamma san or pappa san of the brothel.   One of my sweetest memories is of a visitor from abroad gazing with admiration at the handsome wooden façade of one of these houses, and finding in it confirmation of his belief that Japan was essentially more civilized than degenerate Europe.   It was left to me to persuade the tough old woman whose function is to draw in customers by her mellifluous tongue or her powerful arm that my companion's admiration was strictly architectural.   Strictly academic.[1]

The houses are certainly attractive—the entrance hall in particular is quite enticing—and they have an air of solidity which few Japanese domestic structures can claim.   As for ' civilization ', the licensed quarters are obviously more pleasant and less hypocritical than the pavements of Piccadilly. Pleasure is their purpose : and the members of the profession do not believe that by working upon their clients' sense of sin

[1] At their far end the quarters terminated in a Buddhist shrine compound, which my companion hesitated to enter, on the grounds that the neighbours might take exception to a foreigner polluting the sacred precincts.   I am glad to say that they take no exception to foreigners entering either their brothels or their holy places.

they will obtain better rewards. Nevertheless, one still has an uneasy feeling that women who sell their flesh should be able both to make a little more out of it and to retain a certain independence. The magazine *Kaizō* (April, 1954) carried an article by Mr. Einosuke Itō on the traffic in flesh in the northern provinces of Japan. The writer investigated thirty-two cases of girls sold as geisha apprentices or prostitutes for sums ranging from ¥10,000 to ¥100,000 (£10–100). He found that twenty-one of the girls were under eighteen years of age, and that twenty-three of them had middle school diplomas. In each case the ' broker ' received twenty per cent of the price as his commission.

Regular medical examination renders the *jorō* less ' dangerous ' than the lower species of geisha, since the latter, not being ' prostitutes ', are exempt from such examination. However, the man who marries an ex-*jorō* is letting himself in for trouble : the neighbours will behave maliciously towards her, gossiping and tittering into their sleeves. A woman with ' a past ', an ex-geisha or ex-prostitute, is termed *sore-sha*, literally ' that-person '. It is said that children are rarely born of such unions : the master or mistress of the brothel makes the *jorō* drink some daily ' medicine ' which results in sterility.

Even so, there is something ' traditional ' about the *jorō* : as in the case of *Kabuki*, time has honoured her to some extent. The entertainment world of Japan is a rigid hierarchy : and on the lowest rung are the *pan-pan*, the street-walkers (the term is said to derive from a Malayan word for ' woman ', though many other etymologies have been proposed). The *pan-pan* lack all traditions, poor dears, because they are a post-war phenomenon. When I was out one night with a Japanese teacher we passed a *pan-pan* in urgent conversation with a Japanese youth. My friend groaned heavily : ' A dreadful thing ! A dreadful thing ! One never saw it before the war ! ' He was quite correct—but I felt that his sorrowful indignation was a little exaggerated. No doubt it is more ' civilized ' to restrict such women to the licensed quarters ; whether it is also more moral—and my friend was a moralist—is another matter. It would not be true to say that the Occupation troops brought about the phenomenon of *pan-pan*. It was the war that did it. For us it is difficult to realize how many families lost everything in the bombing, how utterly inadequate were the relief measures, and how many girls went on the streets out of sheer necessity. Japan had no Citizens' Advice Bureaux—but they had the tradition which advised a young girl that she could with merit sell her body to feed her parents. The G.I.s—excluded from the select brothels and despised as barbarians by the geisha *okāsan*—were also on the streets, and the ensuing fraternization must have been the smoothest that history has known. Those Japanese (and it must be said that they are few) who complain that their womenfolk have been corrupted might be reminded that unconsciously they themselves prepared their women for this very task of solacing the Occupation forces—by their emphasis on or at least condonement of obedience, docility and subservience to the male and by their discouragement of pride in women.

Neither America nor Japan can claim to have seen the best side of each other : but they should be glad that this aspect of Occupation was conducted in a spirit kindlier and more quiet than one could have expected. Even today it is not uncommon to see a *pan-pan* administering to a very sick U.S. sailor or soldier, where the average western whore would have picked his pocket and pushed him into the gutter. Troops on Rest and Recuperation leave from Korea—coloured men in particular—often go steady with one girl during their stay in Japan : they thus spend their time and dollars on little outings, in cinemas and in shops (where presumably their girl-friends get commission), and the city enjoys a peacefulness which otherwise might be shattered.

Under the circumstances it seems to me that decent Japanese might be less readily censorious about the activities of the *pan-pan*. Why, the poor girls are commonly rumoured to be Korean (that is, not really Japanese at all).

I have gone too far here in identifying the G.I. girl-friends with the *pan-pan*, perhaps—though it is difficult to see what the former can do now that the supply of ' steady ' G.I.s is running out. Nevertheless, true romances have begun under inauspicious conditions, and I do not like the Japanese habit of thinking in strict and watertight categories—it will not do in this changing world. It is to be hoped that some of them read and digested this sad letter which was printed recently in the daily *English Mainichi* :

I am an American soldier, who has recently married a Japanese girl, and since our marriage some of my views have changed for the worse.

Before our marriage I had a great liking for the Japanese people, and Japan itself, and I had considered staying in Japan after my time in the service was over, for an indefinite time. One of the primary reasons for this was in consideration for my Japanese bride, and so that my children would have a chance to get acquainted with their Japanese grand-parents and their mother's homeland. But now I wouldn't stay in Japan, or let my family stay in Japan, if our lives depended upon it. . . .

My wife and I have done much travelling in Japanese transportation here in Tokyo and I have been looked at with amazement by the Japanese people whenever I offered my seat to one who may need it more than I. My wife is pregnant, and it is very plain to see, but she has had to stand in a train all the way from Ueno station to Tokyo station several times. I have yet to see the much talked of ' Oriental courtesy ' that is so much talked of in America.

My wife who had known no man before me, which seems to be hard for people to believe because I am a soldier, has been called a ' whore ' by her own people on the streets of Tokyo (yes, Japanese people) who should know better because she is very large with child in the first place, and in the second place, she has a perfect right as a free and decent citizen to marry whomever she pleases, regardless of what country he is from.

We cannot walk anywhere together without having fifty per cent of the Japanese people staring at us as though we are freaks of some sort, and talk of us within our hearing. . . .

Now, sir, I wish to make one thing clear. I don't hold the Japanese people completely at fault, because being a soldier I realize that there isn't much respect due, because of the way that the average soldier acts in a country away from his homeland. But the Japanese people should realize too that their own soldiers acted the same as we have, when they were in other countries such as China and Korea.

Being a country that has seen much hardships, Japan should be just a bit more broad-minded than she is. . . .

In most other countries that girl would have been given the benefit of the doubt.   But here things are defined in advance, people know what to ' expect ' : the *sensei* is an austere if not melancholy thinker who doesn't know one end of a bottle (or a woman) from the other ; a politician is a god to be obeyed or a devil to be assassinated ; a poet is a superior and useless being who lives on moon-viewing and rice (and the poet who gets drunk is definitely Chinese) ; a *pan-pan* is a non-Japanese because street-walking is not a Japanese tradition ; and a girl who goes about with a foreign soldier is necessarily a whore. . . .   The Japanese are generally tolerant in their everyday behaviour—they would not throw anything at the girl, they would not sack a *sensei* because he was given to merriment—but they are rarely tolerant in their thinking.   However, society is in the melting-pot, and these narrow traditional ways of judging behaviour and motive must eventually yield to habits of thought which are both more realistic and more liberal.

Little fleas have littler fleas : even the *pan-pan*, whose stock in trade amounts only to a few square feet of *tatami* (floor mats of tightly bound rice-straw), usually works for a mamma san, who takes the money.   There may well be something of the mother-daughter relationship in it : the girl helps to keep the older woman, the older woman keeps an eye on the health of the girl.   Although at the moment the supply of this commodity seems to exceed the demand, there is little evidence of price-cutting, so possibly the mamma san belong to an informal union.   The odd thing to our way of thinking is the absence of any intrigue by the girls against the mamma san—capital and labour seem to be firmly at one here. But behind the little fleas stand the human lice, the big 'bosses' who control whole districts, pull the necessary strings and take fifty per cent of the *pan-pans'* earnings. The central government is too weak to tackle this ancient cancer; the local authorities are paralysed by the influence which the 'bosses' command and by their readiness to use physical violence against would-be reformers.

I remember one night passing a *pan-pan* in the street. Feeling unusually benign, I answered her half-hearted invitation with '*Iie, sumimasen*'—'Excuse me, but no.' She understood '*sumimasen*' by its other, related, meaning of 'thank you', and at once fell into an ecstasy of embarrassment. 'No!' she cried after me, imploringly, as she hopped from one foot to the other in her sheer inadequacy, 'No say "thank you", no say "thank you"!' Such supposed politeness was more than she could complacently accept. Indeed, we were both rather moved.

9 : UNSUCCESSFUL SINNERS

In the *Kojiki*, one of the two 'holy books' of Shinto, the story is told of how Izanagi, the world-maker, failed in his attempt to rescue his wife from the world of the dead. He made the mistake of looking upon her before she was ready for him, and he saw that she was a mass of putrescence. In proper feminine indignation Izanami chased him back, whereupon the distressed husband began to pronounce the words of divorce. Izanami threatened him : 'If thou dost so, in one day will I strangle to death one thousand of thy people.' Izanagi replied : 'If thou dost so, I will cause in one day to be born fifteen hundred. . . .' The two original gods seem to have set a pace which has been followed ever since : in Japan most things happen on a large scale.

The saying in Kobe is that every week a hundred little bars go bankrupt and a hundred and one new little bars start up. These bars may not be 'traditionally' Japanese, but they are certainly *sui generis*. They are managed by a mamma san, and staffed by young women whose function is to pour out the customer's drink, perhaps help him to drink it or in other ways encourage him to order more, listen to his stories, play dice or dance with him and otherwise keep him entertained. The bigger bars sometimes boast a boy san ; the smaller ones may have room for no more than three hostesses and three customers.

A bottle of Japanese beer in the shops costs ¥113 (about 2s. 4d.) ; in these bars the price is generally ¥200 or ¥250 (4s. or 5s.). These prices may alarm the patron of the English pub ; but he should remember that in a Japanese bar one gets a good deal more attention, of one kind or another, than in

the average English public house.   In Japan the bar-maids
actually behave as if they were glad to see you.

These bars go in for ' the personal touch ', and generally
the volume of their trade is not large.   They survive because
they supply a social need in this period of transition ; they
seem to be the middle-income-man's ' entertainment ', for
the girls are clearly what we might call ' utility geisha '.   The
pattern of behaviour is perhaps less elevated than that of the
geisha party, but it is more realistic, more human and more
honest :   the formal opening, the mutually respectful conversation between customers and ' hostesses ', the fairly
speedy relaxation, the pawing and the horseplay (with the
girls striving to defend themselves without offending the
customers, or giving up one of those aims according to their
tastes), and the unsteady departure of the customer, with or
more often without one of the girls.

The bars are financed by *sake* breweries or by loan organizations who claim a small sum back—every day in the case of
small and precarious bars, and every month in the case of
more ambitious enterprises.   The profit made by the average
mamma san is not likely to be large, but one perquisite is that
she (and perhaps her girls) can doss down on the sofas at
night and thus save the charge of maintaining lodgings.   The
bar industry, all the same, is a large one and, like the geisha
industry, it has many ramifications.   It helps to support such
ancillary professions as taxi-drivers, fortune-tellers, prostitutes,
shoe-shine boys, flower-sellers (usually children, sometimes
four and five years old, who get ten per cent of the takings
from their bosses), itinerant musicians such as flute-players
and guitarists (some of the bigger bars employ a pianist,
while the ' night clubs ' sport a small ' combo '), artists
(students who go from bar to bar in the hope of sketching a
charitable customer), bar touts who distribute their alluring
little cards complete with map in the streets of the neighbourhood, and no doubt others too.

But the distinguishing feature of these Japanese bars, small
and large, is the ' hostess '—or, as I shall hereafter less

euphemistically call her, the bar-girl.   These girls generally
receive ¥10,000 (£10) per month, upwards to ¥50,000 in
successful Tokyo establishments of the plush variety.   It is
said that the Number One girls of the biggest cabarets, fre-
quented mainly by business men, make as much as ¥70,000
to ¥100,000 per month : that is to say, well over twice as
much as the occupant of a Chair in a first-grade university.
The arrangement at such places is that when a customer spends
more than £100 in one night the girl assigned to him will
get ten per cent of this sum as an extra bonus—so it will be
understood that such girls are exceptionally lucky, even taking
into account the amount they will have to spend on clothes.
The great majority make little more than £10 in the month.
A Japanese writer cites the case of Miss Hiroe, ' a popular and
well-paid waitress ' at the ' Jung Frau ' on the Ginza : ' She
is a war widow with two daughters and a mother whom she
has to support.   She was a salaried girl at a book-store once
but could not afford to support her family on the income she
made then.   Now her income at the cabaret is enough to
support her family, but still not enough to insure her future.
Her only worry is that her working life holds no guarantee
against old age and other unforeseen occurrences.'   But Miss
Hiroe is no more representative of the Japanese bar-girl
profession than blistered feet are representative of the horrors
of modern warfare.

What is the background of these girls ?   ' Any woman can
find such a job,' says the same writer, ' provided she is prepared
to display and disport her sex to the full.'   He also states that
women enter the profession in most cases ' as a last resort
after having suffered some misery such as the death of their
husbands, a divorce or a betrayal in love '.   That is all very
poetical, and it may apply to some of the hostesses working
in the more expensive cabarets.   But the overwhelming reason
is that which forces women into the brothels and on to the
streets—the economic reason.[1]   Firstly, it is not so very easy

[1] A secondary reason for prostitution advanced in the Japanese
press is the absence of normal marital relations in a rather large

for a girl to find a respectable job ; secondly, having found one, she may be working long hours for a small wage. At least the hours of the bar-girl extend only from 6 p.m. to 1 a.m., though some bars will stay open just as long as there is a customer present. And in fact the bar-girls often do have another job which they perform in the daytime : a fact which accounts for the lack of vivacity which sometimes sets in towards midnight. (A humane customer will not make a scene if the girl who is entertaining him drops off to sleep for ten minutes or so ; he will not be resentful if he finds that the girl he is dancing with is asleep on her feet : the Japanese have the gift of taking cat-naps under the most discouraging conditions.) As I mentioned earlier, Japanese universities have no adequate scholarship system, for all the democratic spirit they display where ' standards ' are concerned ; and occasionally a girl who is working her way through college will put in six or seven hours of unacademic activity in some such bar at nights. In a fairly high-class cabaret girl students receive ¥350 (7s.) per day and, after an apprenticeship of one month, a fixed monthly salary of £4 10s., tips, if any, extra.

On top of what the bar-girl receives from the mamma san she keeps her tips and she may make more by sleeping with the customers after the bar has closed. Arrangements differ regarding this extra-mural work. Sometimes the mamma san takes the money herself from the customer : for instance, in humble circumstances she may receive 14s., of which she gives 8s. to the girl and pockets the rest. In other cases the girl gives the mamma san 10s. as she leaves the bar with the customer, so that she will gain whatever she can make above that amount.

proportion of cases. There is said to be considerable homosexuality in the country at present, and considerable lesbianism. The latter strikes the eye ; one wonders whether this, and the great popularity of the Girls' Opera, are not a kind of protest against the lingering assumption of male superiority. Conservative critics would rather put it down to the disastrous tampering with the traditional family system, of course.

There are of course many bar-girls who do not supplement their earnings in this way.   Then, too, some only sleep with the customers they choose to;   while others, particularly those working in the bigger cabarets, become the mistresses of native and foreign business men.   The girl's wishes on this matter will be respected by the mamma san, or else she is free to go elsewhere;   whatever the vicissitudes of her work, she is at least not *sold* to her employer.

Whether or not they are in fact prostitutes, bar-girls are not officially so considered, and they are therefore not subject to medical examination for venereal diseases.   However, they must obtain a certificate of medical clearance on the grounds that they are engaged in the purveyance of food.   This is primarily to exclude serious cases of T.B., but it becomes both simple and unexceptionable to check on V.D. at the same time—and thus a degree of medical control is kept over those who are purveying other things than food and drink.

In nature these bars range from the kind which caters for Japanese only to the kind which aims at a specifically foreign clientele.   The proportion of girls who prostitute themselves is higher in the latter than in the former;   prices are apt to be higher too, and the girls will speak a form of English.   The ' Japanese only ' bar is ' off limits ' of its own desire, to keep out the foreign military devils;   and a civilian foreigner may be made to feel definitely unwelcome unless he is introduced as the guest of a Japanese *habitué*.   In my limited experience, these are the most genteel of the bars;   the girls may not speak English but their voices will be all the softer.   And their behaviour will be more modest (that is, coyer)—for modesty, they know, tickles Japanese masculinity, whereas boldness is what appeals to foreigners.   The ' foreigners' bar ', at its most extreme, is rather disagreeable.   The gentle Japanese maiden is transformed into a hard-faced, hard-voiced gold-digger : at any rate comparatively speaking, for compared with the run of respectable British bar-maids she is still something of a shrinking violet.   And the rattle of dollars is always annoying, for those who possess none.

Between the two extremes you will find many bars which are patronized by Japanese and foreigners alike. Such places are the pleasantest of the lot and often very amusing. Relations between Japanese and foreign customers are generally warm. The first approaches come from the Japanese, who are inclined to yield to the softening effects of alcohol more speedily. In a mixture of English and Japanese and sign-language the new acquaintance is cross-examined : ' You are American ? ', ' You are business man ? ', ' How old ? ', ' Married ? ', ' How many children ? ', ' You like Japanese beer/Japanese *sake*/Japanese *musumesan* (Miss Daughter) ? ', etc. Cards are exchanged. And frequently the Japanese will insist on making some little present to his friend : a packet of cigarettes or a drink. Then with much wringing of hands and slapping of backs they part, probably never to meet again. The exchange of cards is *de rigueur* here, as elsewhere in Japanese society : offering one's card to one particular customer suddenly brings others out of their corners and even off the floor or out of some girl's lax embrace, all proffering their cards in exchange. The next morning one finds one's pockets full of them, and not the slightest notion of which belonged to whom, which was the one who wanted to take you to *Kabuki* or a nude show, which it was who invited you to visit his office, which was the person who offered to sell you a camera or a washing machine at cost price . . .

Misbehaviour in the bars is usually limited to going a bit far with the girls (which the mamma san will stop, tactfully, just at the crucial moment), dancing drunkenly, laughing uproariously at puns and other witticisms, and falling on the floor. It is amusing to notice how a party of Japanese, invariably middle-aged, who have been extremely noisy, pull themselves together, pay their bill or sign their chit quietly, take a final farewell and leave in good order. The Japanese tend to get drunk quickly, it is true—but they generally sober up quickly, too. It all seems like an exercise of will-power. They relax their will and sink into inebriation and somewhat

childish horseplay.   Suddenly the hour has struck, they apply
their will and lift themselves back wholesale into cold and
slightly shame-faced sobriety, all the responsibilities of
tomorrow settling on their shoulders already.   The foreigner
of normally strong head in a Japanese party is apt to feel even
censoriously sober at first : the company seems to be going to
pieces in front of his eyes.   He may find however that he
takes considerably longer to sober up than the others.   The
next day, when he is suffering from a physical hangover, his
Japanese companions are more likely to be suffering from a
slight moral one—their consciences are pricking them.   For
though ' relaxation ' may be permitted in the scheme of things
from time to time, yet it is not proper to think tolerantly of
' relaxation ' when not in the actual state thereof.

I have never witnessed any violence or any of those fights
outside which disfigure English Saturday nights around
closing time.   For outward decorousness the bar areas of
Japanese ports compare well with those of our better policed
English ones.   When irrevocably drunk, Japanese are prone
to get sick—which is a nuisance—but they do not turn nasty.
They either become sentimental or go to sleep.   Any cut-
throat element there may be will probably have been introduced by transitory foreign seamen, and even they generally
succumb to the beneficently feminine influence of the ladies.
At present Japanese policemen are reluctant to get mixed up
with foreigners ; the mamma san may threaten to call in her
big brother but the odds are that he, if he exists, will prefer
to stay out of trouble.   In a mumble of half-hearted recriminations and explanations and excuses all mixed up with the
soothing noises of the girls, the affair usually dies out.   It
is difficult to kick up hell in face of the passive resistance of the
Japanese, especially when they are female.

The standard of honesty in the bars is remarkably high,
once you accept the standard prices : one pays for what one
(and perhaps one's ' hostess ') has drunk, and a new customer
is often told the price of the drinks before he orders.   It may
happen that the mamma san adds a little to the bill—but very

rarely, and only in the case of foreigners unknown to her. While talking to the mamma san of the Bar Rimbaud on my first and last visit there, I was astounded to gather that she sent her daughter to the kindergarten attached to the university where I was working—possibly the most select and probably the most expensive Japanese kindergarten in the country. This visit was the only one in my experience which terminated in an argument over the bill. It is practically impossible to keep count of the small jars in which *sake* is served. Finally we managed to get ten per cent knocked off— this being a so-called ' service charge '—on the grounds that the mamma san and her one assistant had remained throughout on their side of the bar.

The honesty of the average bar-girl is even embarrassing. One would feel happier, perhaps, could one dismiss her as a deceitful bitch. The solicitude which the girls show for an utterly incapable and peculiarly unprepossessing drunkard marks them out as born for wifehood, motherhood or a nursing career. They will pick him up off the floor, brush him down, hold his head, gather the banknotes he has scattered over the floor and restore them all to his wallet, and then haul him tenderly to the nearest taxi. They themselves generally remain sober ; they are very conscious of the fact that alcohol quickly brings an unsightly flush to their faces, and in some bars the drinks bought for them contain little alcohol. It happens sometimes, however, that one of the girls is having a night out—her occasional ' relaxation ', as it were—and she will be as noisy as any of the men and almost as sportive. In that case the other girls will keep an uncensorious eye on her. Passions do not run high among them, and their solidarity is impressive. Not one would dream of stealing another's favourite customer ; equally not one would think of deserting the customer she is entertaining in favour of her particular friend unless an exchange is agreeable to him. The customer, whether a favourite or not, must be seen off at the door, with many thanks for his honourable patronage and the warm invitation, ' *Dōzo, mata irasshai, ne ?* ' (' Please come again, won't you ? ')—a phrase which one rarely hears on the lips of English publicans.

In short, the Japanese almost succeed in making a rather dusty trade, or cluster of trades, look cleaner than straight-forward English boozing. At the very outset, the pleasant exterior, the conviction with which one is welcomed, the readiness to cope unquestioningly with any of one's little eccentricities—all this tends to steal the thunder with which one might be prepared to denounce the whole complicated machinery of night-life. Night-life goes on in abundance : it comes in all sizes, to suit all purses and all perversions ; and it is easy of access. Yet there is a strange absence of real viciousness. Men who frequent brothels do so without any present sense of guilt—perhaps because it has always been done, perhaps because it proves that a man is a man and not tied to his wife's kimono-strings. They behave all the better, in this pursuit, through suffering from no sense of guilt. (Though the Japanese read with reverence the words of T. S. Eliot, they have in general not managed to achieve what he described as man's glory—' his capacity for damnation '). The women who provide the pleasure are clean and neatly dressed, they make every effort to ensure the customer's comfort and even do so as if they really meant it ; they bow him in, they accept the agreed sum without haggling for more and even with the expression of gratitude, and they bow him out. An ordinary business transaction has taken place in a calm atmosphere.

I imagine that, in spite of the amount of prostitution in Japan, there is less ' viciousness ' in the whole of the country than can be found in the immediate environs of Piccadilly or Place Pigalle. The point is that the inclinations of these women lie in the direction of the domestic virtues, and those virtues will out, whatever the circumstances may be. Their attempts to achieve an ' exciting ' viciousness are rarely successful : they would much rather give up the effort and just be nice. I have noticed no signs here of that *nostalgie de la boue* which is said to be one of the contributory reasons why women in other

7. Red-light District.

8. A cluster of bars, Kyoto.

countries go into prostitution.   The Japanese gentleman too
lays greater store by the domestic virtues, whatever the circumstances, than we do.   On his night out he likes to be mothered
a bit.   I have heard of the existence of places catering for this
desire—places where a tired middle-aged man can go, to eat
some well-prepared little delicacy and drink in moderation,
either nicely cooled beer or nicely warmed *sake*, while a
middle-aged woman, skilled in the understanding of the male
creature, calms his fevered brow, tells him everything he wants
to hear, and sends him home feeling a new man.   It is difficult
for us to realize how highly self-conscious the average Japanese
male is—and how much in the way of soothing unguents he
therefore requires to lay to himself.

The ambition, which bar-girls share with geisha, to run a
little bar in their retirement, might seem a strange one, worth
a moment's consideration.   There are already so many bars
that no one is likely to make a fortune out of it ; and it is hard
work.   But it is work in which these women are already skilled
—in brief, the tactful management of the male.   The ambition
to have a bar of one's own seems to correspond to the desire
for a home of one's own among other women.   Moreover,
the mamma san reigns supreme in her bar and she is a person
of some consequence in the neighbourhood—the Japanese
wife does not always reign supreme in her home ; though
her husband is content to leave domestic affairs in her
hands, the dreaded mother-in-law may insist on her ancient
prerogative.

Why do young girls whose standard of intelligence is
reasonably high go into the ' hostess ' profession in the first
case ?   The question may be answered by a brief look at what
they would gain elsewhere.   The average monthly income of a
working girl has been estimated at ¥8,140, that is, £8 3s.,
with the highest getting £15 and the lowest £4 10s.   According to the same estimate, seventy per cent of these girls live
with their parents and contribute an average of £2 4s. to the
family coffer.   An average of £2 7s. is spent on clothes ;
17s. on extra food and drinks ; 15s. on books and magazines ;

I

13*s.* on social expenses (whatever they may be); 11*s.* on entertainment; 7*s.* 6*d.* on chemist's items; and 5*s.* on cosmetics. The other thirty per cent rent rooms, either because they can afford it or because they have no relatives; in the latter case, it is clear that many of them must somehow increase their earnings. The path of virtue, for those of poor family background, is not an easy one to follow.

The figures are especially interesting in that the sum spent on books and magazines is proportionately high. Japan is rich in magazines of the *Picture Post* variety, and people of moderate and low income are more ready to spend money on books than are their better-off social equivalents in England. Fashion magazines and magazines devoted to photography are particularly numerous, but even in the poorer-class areas you will come across shop after shop containing nothing but piles of magazines, many of general interest.[1]

[1] As of December 1953 Japanese magazines in regular publication totalled 1,201 (including 965 monthlies), and the number has increased since then. Fiction is what sells, of course, and it sells on a vast scale. *Heibon*, a monthly given up to fiction, enjoys a circulation of over a million copies; the standard of the contents is indicated by its title, 'Mediocrity'. A rather more serious monthly, *Bungei Shunjū* (first published in January 1923 under the editorship of the dramatist, Kan Kikuchi), which prints essays on general topics as well as a large proportion of fiction, sells 600,000 copies. The magazines of a higher intellectual order are all leftist politically, in varying degrees. Conservatives govern the country, but socialists govern the book-shops.

Worthy of mention is a monthly magazine of a more professional nature, *Eigo Seinen* (with the English title, *The Rising Generation*), which is devoted to English and American literary and linguistic studies. Founded in April 1898 and at present edited by the distinguished professor and scholar of English, Rintarō Fukuhara, *Eigo Seinen* is bilingual and has always been hospitable to foreign teachers in Japan. One of its features is the 'letter from England' in which some Japanese professor recounts the interviews he has had with F. R. Leavis in Cambridge and F. W. Bateson in Oxford or relates the latest literary gossip from London. The magazine

The sum allocated to clothes is also significant. Japanese
girls dress so neatly (in, say, fairly cheap Japanese imitations
of the more amenable Paris fashions) that foreigners are often
deceived into assuming that their stomachs must be full.   It
is clear from the figures—and from their reactions to the offer
of a free meal—that many of them, especially those who do
not share in a family table, are eating no more than the bare
minimum.[1]   The importance placed on a tidy appearance
pervades the nation (it is a little less pronounced among males) ;
a bar-girl will bear any amount of amorous pinching with
fortitude, but should her precious blouse get torn, the fat will
really be in the fire.

But to return to the main subject of this chapter.   It is
easy for a foreigner to wax indignant at this involved apparatus
of pleasure-seeking.   It is also easy for the foreigner, particularly if he is a refugee from Anglo-Saxon drinking habits,
to be seduced by the veneer of ' civilization ' which it wears.
What I have tried to do, perhaps unsuccessfully, is to show
something of the complex mixture of good and bad, gentleness
and callousness, humanity and inhumanity, self-expression
and frustration, which makes up the whole.   I have not been
concerned with the abstract ' morality ' of the entertainment
industry.   What is appalling is the wastage of human lives,
of valuable human gifts.   In case I have not conveyed the
sheer *volume* of that wastage, here are some extracts from an
editorial on prostitution which appeared in a recent (November
1954) issue of the *Tokyo Times* :

Under instructions from SCAP, GHQ, the Japanese Government
abolished public prostitution after the war, but this only resulted

---

has a healthy circulation among teachers and students of English
and steers a useful course between academicism and popularization.

[1] According to a Welfare Ministry survey covering April 1953—
March 1954, twenty-three per cent of the population were undernourished.   I do not know where the boundary is fixed, but on
impression I should have thought nearly twice that percentage more
accurate.

in increasing the number of unlicensed prostitutes. Prostitutes began to walk the streets of Tokyo, and finally as an inevitable measure, the red-light districts had to be recognized so as to cater to the Occupation Forces.

The licensed prostitution districts had previously been strictly separated, but the new orders resulted in the houses of ill repute calling themselves 'special restaurants' and the prostitutes 'hostesses', making it extremely difficult to differentiate between them and legitimate restaurants.

That is why there are now 'blue-light districts' as against 'red-light' districts and the field of activity of prostitutes is being enlarged without restrictions. . . . It would be no exaggeration to say that never before has Japan been so immoral . . .

The majority of the estimated 600,000 prostitutes in the country are barely eking out a living. They know the baseness of their calling, but there is no other place to work and earn money. Prostitution can be controlled and prostitutes can be punished only after their rehabilitation is planned and their living is guaranteed.

No, the would-be reformer has no right to cry out against the sinfulness of it unless he can propose a solution to the essential problem—the problem that we return to time and time again, whatever the context. So many people, rich in energy and perseverance, crowded into so small a space, and lacking worthy outlets for their energy. The ways of tradition do provide a sort of outlet—we have seen how this strange system of measured mutual help extends from the business house which patronizes a particular tea-house right through to the *samisen* teacher and the taxi-driver. It is comparable to the old paternalism of Japanese employers. But at the same time it has a paralysing effect : the pattern repeats itself ; it carries no sufficient guarantee. It is certainly no substitute for the kind of social security which we knew in Britain even before we gave it that name.

It is useless to talk of closing the brothels until you have opened other doors. Can other doors be opened until the notion of female inferiority, a notion sustained by the brothels, has been rooted out ? I see no simple and quick solution to Japan's social problem. When there is so much flesh available, then flesh will sell cheaply—unless there exists a strong sense of human dignity at all levels. That sense exists only sporadically at present, but it is growing in strength. Another war would kill it dead—but then, that goes for the rest of the world, too. It seems that we are all in the same boat.

TRAFFIC REGULATIONS

Soothingly, soothingly go in the grease mud,
    where there is lurking the big skid demon.
Softly, into the bar slip softly, for there
    the corpses stand and lie.
Slowly, go with the maidens slowly, for they
    are human,
Though they smile, whose only reason is to cry—

For crippled husbands, useless virtues, ruined
    fathers, vain diplomas.
Gently, when your dancing partners gently fall
    and fall asleep upon their feet.
Yet you surely serve them, surely, since your
    whiskey breath and garlic rumours
Mean for them a meal, who might not eat.

Then promptly pay your portion, sadly say your
    sayonara, weakly wish them some dim maybe—
See, a little knowledge, little pity, knocks your
    sex upon its head.
Give big space to festive dog in slender roadway,
    sleeping beggar, straying baby,
Roll respected, roll respectable, roll respectful
    home to bed.

10 : SOME MYTHS ABOUT NIPPON

> ' The Japanese are in general intelligent and
> provident, free and unconstrained, obedient
> and courteous, curious and inquisitive,
> industrious and ingenious, frugal and sober,
> cleanly, good-natured and friendly, upright
> and just, trusty and honest, mistrustful,
> superstitious, proud, and haughty, un-
> forgiving, brave and invincible.'
> (*Travels in Europe, Africa, and Asia,*
> *performed between the years 1770 and*
> *1779*', *Vol. III, by Charles Peter*
> *Thunberg, M.D.*)

THE Japanese are a highly self-conscious people, and hence
highly conscious of the opinions which foreigners hold concerning them and their country. They certainly have the
gift of seeing themselves through other people's eyes—even
through the eyes of people for whom they have little respect.
And they see no point in disturbing the myths regarding
Japan and the Japanese which foreign visitors bear about them.
There is a good deal of politeness in this ; it is indeed ' Japanese politeness ' which is evinced in their effort to live up to
these foreign preconceptions. It is not hypocrisy : there is
in fact something of humility about it. At the same time, the
habit can be exasperating to anyone who wishes to see the
Japanese as they are and not merely as they think he wishes
to see them. The present chapter concerns some of these
foreign myths—foreign in their provenance, though fostered
and encouraged by the Japanese themselves.

JAPANESE MANNERS

The gap between private manners and public behaviour is so wide and deep that many a foreigner's incipient love for Japan has died a violent or a lingering death in it. Of private manners it is sufficient to say that they are as near perfect as makes no matter. The guiding principle is not mere attention to form, for the Japanese will display a positive ingenuity in his determination to make a guest comfortable. Those foreigners who find Japanese politeness an empty and unfeeling form might be asked what exactly they expect in the way of manners. A kick in the backside to show the fullness of the host's heart? A booby trap at the door to make the guest feel that he is one of the family? The Englishman and the American in particular make a fetish of what is called ' casualness '—the Japanese would consider casualness to be open rudeness, and my sympathies are rather with him. We Anglo-Saxons are too ready to see something ' sinister ' in polite and thoughtful behaviour.

Unfortunately Japanese manners seem to be peculiar to personal relations, and they incline to die a sudden death in the ruder atmosphere of public life. For our field of study we might take one of the commonest forms of public life and, for those who have no car, the least escapable—the suburban electric train.

Perhaps you start at the head of a queue, waiting for the train to come in. But you will find that queuing operates in reverse, and you are soon firmly established at the back of a seething mob. The rush, the silent struggle for seats, is almost frightening. Should you have a young child with you, a woman may offer her seat : a man will not be likely to do so, even for a woman in her tenth month. Students and schoolboys are the most determined seat-seekers and the most tenacious seat-keepers : it is as if some certain disgrace attaches to strap-hanging. Little boys are especially dangerous in that they will dart between your legs to scramble on a seat, or part of one which they soon make their own ; once there they open the windows and bounce about energetically and, quite unintentionally of course, wipe their shoes and their running noses on the clothes of their neighbours. No one dares to say a word : little boys are privileged. Little girls generally behave very well : they are not privileged. At every stop people push in, with a set neutral and hardly human expression on their faces which is not pleasant to see ; and there is usually a collision at the door between those intending to enter and those attempting to leave. This ridiculous disobedience towards a law of nature always enrages me. When an empty train comes in to start its run, even though thirty people are queuing for each coach of over sixty seats, precisely the same thing happens : one is slashed by bundles of blossoming thorn-tree, battered by bulging brief-cases and sharp-cornered fish-crates, and stabbed with umbrellas.

My stoicism falling short of Japanese standards, eventually I remonstrated shortly with some man, pushing in as I was trying to get out, who had stepped heavily on my foot (*geta*, the wooden clogs, can do a lot of damage).[1] The effect was astounding. If I had promptly turned him into a frog he could not have been more surprised. I was conscious too of the cold and incredulous gaze of bystanders. To push back is in order—it should be done as impersonally as possible ; if you trample some old woman who is tugging a bundle bigger than herself, that too is accepted, even by the victim. But to protest by word or gesture against being needlessly shoved about—that is a gross offence against the non-existent manners of travelling, it is unheard-of, it is altogether ' unexpected '. One is arrogating to oneself the public opinion

[1] Lafcadio Hearn remarked that the shoe ' has distorted the Western foot out of the original shape, and rendered it incapable of the work for which it was evolved ' (*Kokoro*). The *geta* has precisely the same effect—on other people's feet. Judging from the general ugliness of Japanese feet (in sharp contrast to the hands, which are frequently beautiful), Hearn was here, as often elsewhere, failing to see clearly what was under his nose.

which, alas, practically fails to exist. I really think that the greatest trial which the foreigner in Japan is subject to is the co-existence of an enormous stoicism alongside an enormous absence of the public opinion which could so easily eradicate some of the country's persistent irritations.

The ' last train ' is sometimes the most and sometimes the least amusing. Once when I was travelling on the last train from Kyoto to Kobe, a drunken and energetic young man burst into the coach, removed his shirt (to display a most intricate expanse of tattooing), flung it dexterously on to the luggage rack and proceeded to sit heavily on the laps of the female passengers. No one did anything about it. They just sat and looked dispassionately, or—like those on whom he was sitting—pretended not to notice anything. Finally my fascinatingly long nose caught his attention and he stag-gered over, presumably to test its genuineness. As I lack Japanese forbearance, a nasty situation would have been upon us, had not the young man decided at the very last moment that he only wanted to be friends with me and my nose. It was the rest of the coach that I really felt furious with : they were of the same nationality as he, yet no one told him to shut up or sit down or behave himself. They had simply transported themselves to another and better world. A few minutes later two further drunks entered. One of them loosened his belt, dropped his trousers and rearranged his underwear, all while hanging precariously from the strap. At the next station the two sat down next to me and carried on some noisy and disgruntled but harmless conversation. Suddenly the more responsible of the two became aware of me. In a comic mixture of languages he conveyed his apologies : ' *Sumimasen!* Police catch *tomodachi* in Amaga-saki, *takusan* trouble . . .' He philosophized, ' Japanese man *sukoshi* drinku, *dame desŭ*,' pointing to his head, ' Japa-nese drink a little, and soon no good.' I assured him that he and his friend had not incommoded me in the least. He was so touched that he shot up, removed his cap, bowed several times and offered further apologies. Our exchange of bows and apologies and reassurances and expressions of gratitude continued until I got off the train.

All the same, I had to admit later that this attitude of ' not seeing ' often works out well. The drunk is conscious that he has no audience, either approving or disapproving, he feels that he has been tacitly excluded from society, and his violence fades away into apologies or complaints of misunderstood affection. The showdown is averted. With drunks the system works well on the whole. But where the behaviour of politicians and statesmen is concerned, it is obviously no adequate substitute for public opinion.

It may be that the irrational way in which Japanese treat their impressively efficient railways so disrespectfully is another instance of their tendency to think in watertight compartments. The house is the house, the *tatami* is the sacred *tatami*, and one's behaviour in the one and on the other is restrained and decent. (The sight of foreigners walking in slippers on the *tatami* of their own houses can arouse a mild Japanese housemaid to considerable indignation.) But the train is not the house, and the seats are not *tatami* —therefore the coach is a no man's land to be littered with paper bags, scraps of food, used handkerchiefs and spittle *ad lib*. I must apologize for recounting the following chestnut, but it is still illuminating. In the first days of railways passengers behaved as they would when entering a private house. They discarded their clogs and left them in neat rows on the edge of the platform. On arriving at their destinations they were shocked and aggrieved to discover that the officials had failed to pick them up and bring them along in the guard's van. That cured them. The reaction set in and they flew to the other extreme. The author of a book published in 1904 wrote : ' Enter a second-class car on a Japanese railway after night has fallen and you find the Japanese race unmasked. From a race of pleasant, polite, deprecating folk they are changed to unmitigated boors.' The writer probably had in mind the custom—still common, by day as well as night—of undressing in public transports on long journeys. There is nothing indecent about this—it is a male prerogative (like many other dubious mannerisms) and Japanese males wear a species of combination-suit which covers them effectively from neck to ankles. It could be said, though, that it is aesthetically indecent.

The general rule among the people at large seems to be that where the shoes or clogs are discarded, behaviour is impeccable, and where they are retained, anything goes. Footwear is, as it were, unclean. (It is the case that those who make it are mainly outcasts.) It is common to meet Japanese people, dressed smartly from head to ankle, but wearing on their feet shoes which are swollen, shapeless, down at heel and muddy. However, they are becoming more shoe-conscious these days under the influence of foreign clothing fashions, and it is not inconceivable that as their respect for footwear increases, so their lack of respect for public places may decrease. The Japanese attach more importance to ' symbols ' than to fresh and logical reasoning.

What I have said about public transport applies equally to other non-private establishments. It is disconcerting, in a cinema, to become suddenly aware of a large and naked foot nestling against each of one's ears—even though the foot is likely to be reasonably clean. And it is not as if the Japanese really enjoyed dirt and untidiness. The crowd in an Egyptian cinema get immense satisfaction from scattering melon-seed shells around them and dropping paper bags and cigarette packets on the heads of those in the pit. But Japanese untidiness has an element of the puritanical about it—it is carried on without enjoyment, as if they somehow felt that it wasn't nice but hadn't actually been instructed on the point. Perhaps it is another of those activities in which the Japanese have stifled their better nature in favour of the ' expected '.

It would be unfair not to repeat that in face-to-face dealings, once any kind of personal relationship has been established, courtesy prevails. Even in a not especially high-class restaurant you will receive a modicum of ' personal attention '—a pleasing civility which puts the west to unconditional shame.

JAPANESE CLEANLINESS

As far as the male shirt and the female blouse are concerned, I remarked earlier, cleanliness comes before nourishment. Even if only superficial, cleanliness, in a country so painfully over-crowded, is a virtue which it would be difficult to praise too highly.

Much has already been written about *o furo* (the Japanese bath) and the social behaviour surrounding it. The bath itself is wooden, and generally square in shape ; the water is heated by gas or wood while it is in the bath, and the hotter the temperature the better the Japanese like it. The procedure is for everyone to use the same water in order of precedence, from the guest or else the head of the family down to the youngest daughter or maidservant.

The theory is that one scrubs oneself first, outside the bath, with soap and hot water ; one rinses oneself thoroughly ; and then one enters the bath. Comic stories are told of uninitiated foreigners who committed the cardinal sin of soaping themselves in the bath and thus polluting the water. Quite ridiculous and uncivilized. However, the account of *furo* behaviour which our maid gave us did not quite match with the official story : she told us that firstly one entered the bath, to get warm and perhaps to soften the dirt ; then one got out and scrubbed oneself ; and then one went back in to relax.

A number of foreigners have expressed admiration for the Japanese bath—they have perhaps not lived with one for any length of time. It is true that the wood is pleasant to the touch (much more agreeable than the invincible coldness of enamel) and that the depth of the bath enables one to submerge oneself to the neckline. In these respects it is undeniably superior to the bath as we in the west know it. But the great disadvantage is that the wood quickly collects and retains hairs and pellicles of skin and that, by its shape, it is practically impossible to drain out and clean completely. Baths in hotels often carry upon their surface obvious vestiges of previous customers.

The real justification of the *furo* is that the Japanese people of all social classes find a deep enjoyment in soaking themselves in very hot water.   In winter, particularly in poor households, the children spend much of their life in the bath : it may be the only efficient method of heating they have.   And the cost of preparing fresh water at that temperature for every person would obviously be prohibitive.   In the country, though nearly every house has a bath, the custom is that one bath should be prepared for the use of a group of neighbours ;   each of these in turn extends the hospitality of the *furo* to the others.[1]   The arrangement is logical : the *furo* has provided and still provides one of the greatest of life's pleasures for thousands of poor people.   That should be sufficient reason for its existence :   there is no need to erect around it the precarious edifice of a *furo* mystique.   The only reprehensible thing about the Japanese bath is the conscious ' tourist value ' which it has come to acquire.

As I suggested elsewhere, the Japanese are a myth-making people—a myth-making people deprived of durable mythical heroes.   Hence various sensible ' patterns of behaviour ' and eminently practical *modi vivendi* get embroidered and elevated into pseudo-rituals.   As the educated Japanese is such an intensely self-conscious person these rituals are gradually endowed with a sort of pseudo-philosophy, and a hedge of do's and don'ts, a pseudo-ethics.   And then one ends with something supposed to manifest the unique spirit of Japan.

All nations show this tendency ; but few pursue it as far as the Japanese (who are always ready to learn from foreign sociologists and men of letters).   The unfortunate thing is that this myth-making may swell to the point where the original ' human ' purpose of the activity becomes lost in the fog, vitiated by the un-humanity of the myth and the complicated formality of the ritual.

The sharp division between private and public extends to cleanliness, too : clean people live in dirty streets.   With the

[1] See *Suye Mura : A Japanese Village*, by John F. Embree, Chicago, 1939.

exception of a few ill-kept highways, the streets are straight from Mother Nature, with perhaps a surface sprinkling of treacherous loose pebbles. There is, admittedly, little incentive to keep such streets clean ; and in a country so densely populated, a few dirty people can do a lot of damage. The streets are generally littered with rotting rubbish and dotted with spittle. Water is frequently thrown over them to keep the dust down—at the expense of turning the dust into slippery mud. The paradox remains : much of the life of this country goes on in the little alleys and by-ways, the people squatting down beside their minute shops or their barrows, spitting where they squat (there seems to be an idea that if you smear the ejected spittle with your despised footwear you neutralize its insanitary and otherwise unpleasant elements) and, in the case of men, hardly moving aside to urinate. (One appreciates their reluctance to use the rather primitive *benjo* in their houses, and public lavatories are few and far between and therefore foul.) In brief, the people are cleaner than one would have thought possible, their surroundings more squalid than one could have imagined. How can the former tolerate the latter ?

Untidiness, I am forced to confess, penetrates into the universities. They, like the alleys, are sadly over-populated. Perhaps it is due to lack of attention during the war years that, these days, some part of every university building appears to be under continuous and noisy repair. Alas, the repairs never get finished. When I complained mildly about the wintry cold of the lecture rooms I was told that the heating apparatus had been taken out during the war and not yet replaced. I wonder, though, whether the real reason hasn't to do with the feeling that ' Spartan ' conditions are good for the soul—a proposition partly vitiated by the fact that students and lecturers alike keep their coats on. For in *Suye Mura*, an account of life in a Japanese village published in 1939, John F. Embree wrote, ' There is a confirmed belief that cold and discomfort are good for learning and mental discipline. If any child complains of the cold, the teacher tells him to think of the brave soldiers in Manchukuo, where it is really cold.'

But noise is in season all the year round.   I remember trying to conduct a course on modern English poetry against the relentless competition of an electric railway and a saw-mill outside and a demented carpenter inside.   By good fortune, when my temper finally gave way towards the end of term, there happened to be a helicopter overhead, and so no one's knowledge of the English language was unnaturally enlarged. There simply is no room for the universities in the towns— there is no room for the undergraduates inside the universities —and now, it appears, there is little room for the graduates outside the universities.

Students have to eat in the lecture rooms since there is nowhere else for many of them to go.   Consequently it happens sometimes that the lecturer's profundity is punctuated by the crackling of used chopsticks under his feet.   Perhaps this cannot be helped : the many discomforts which attend higher education these days do not encourage the students to regard their Alma Mater as anything other than a place ' beyond the *tatami* '.   But it passes my understanding why, well in advance of Sports Day, and when students are supposed to be preparing for examinations, people should be allowed to ride motor-cycles outside the classrooms.   This occurred in the same university in which my wife's efforts to teach French were regularly foiled by bugle practice in the room above. I know that the majority of students are hard-working and even excessively serious-minded.   But the whole conception of a university can be reduced to nonsense by the selfish behaviour of a few.   There is no authority over behaviour. The universities, too, seem to be lacking in ' public opinion '.

Would it be preferable to have spick and span students, in full uniform, drawn up at attention when the professor enters, and prepared to swallow their chopsticks rather than drop them in the classrooms ?   Certainly not.   All the same, one can have too much of a good thing . . .

9. Bars and eating-houses, Tokyo.

10. Eating and drinking-stalls, Kyoto.

THE AESTHETIC JAPANESE

At times the Japanese show themselves the most aesthetic people in the world; at others they emerge as the least aesthetic. Unfortunately for the myth, the manifestations of the latter type are the more obtrusive.

Some of the commonest unaesthetic sights and smells are the snotty noses of children (Miss Evelyn Adam, writing in 1910, mentions the missionary lady who exclaimed, ' I wish I had brought a trunk full of handkerchiefs instead of Bibles ! '), the dreary combinations worn by Japanese males, the tawdry heaping of sign upon sign in the streets, the *benjo* smell, the ugly wooden overflowing refuse-boxes which are placed along the streets directly in front of the houses, the uninhibited spitting and hardly inhibited urination.

Against that, there is the universal Japanese gift for colour-matching (except when seduced by foreign bad taste) and, most striking, the gift for the brush and the pencil. My wife used to take lessons in the finer points of horsemanship from a Japanese ex-jockey. When language difficulties reared themselves, he would whip out a pencil and a sheet of paper —and there, in a few strokes, was the horse doing the right thing or my wife doing the wrong thing. He had never had any instruction in art. To write in Chinese characters is itself a little performance in art which even the advent of the necessary fountain-pen has not destroyed. The bamboo, a national symbol and a common art motif, has a natural kinship with the brush used in calligraphy : stroke the brush down the paper and you have the stem of the bamboo, press the brush down at intervals and you have the joints. Almost any Japanese can draw a bamboo in five seconds which in the west could be proudly exhibited as a small and delicate work of art : it seems easy—until one tries it. Then there is the popular art of today : poster-work. The wit, economy and ingenuity of design of Japanese posters make it easier to bear their ubiquitousness.

In music the Japanese seem uninventive ; in literature one

K

may suspect that they are perforce struggling against language and tradition instead of struggling in co-operation with both. But give them something to do with their hands and their eyes and they are truly at home. An ordinary maidservant can arrange a few diced vegetables on a plate with admirable taste, or—without knowing anything, happily, about the mystique of *ikebana* (Japanese Flower Arrangement)—achieve a really refined grouping of three or four common flowers. Similarly, an apparently insensitive person, though he reads nothing more elevating than the newspapers, may exhibit an expert and exquisite taste in ceramics.

Soon after arriving in Japan, I visited an exhibition of ' foreign-style' paintings by Japanese artists. One could pick out the sources of inspiration with distressing ease : this specimen was imitation-Rouault, this Cézanne, this Degas, this Matisse, and this Picasso of some period or other. When those same painters turned to their native style the results seemed impeccable : a waterfall, a crane, a few pine trees, characteristically 'Japanese', unmistakable and absolutely assured. Shortly afterwards I was inveigled into addressing a Japanese cultural club for women, and so I took the opportunity to advise them to stick to the old Japanese style in artistic matters and to avoid western models like the plague. Of course it was rather disappointing to have come all that way only to find remarkably skilful imitations of what one had seen a little too much of at home. But they must have heard that same advice many times before, from Lafcadio Hearn onwards, and they showed no signs of being thrilled by my talk—for which I am profoundly grateful now. For, after all, the ' foreign-style' artists are struggling to escape from an ancient and rather automatic and finally stultifying convention ; and, more important, they are striving, however unoriginally, to deal with human themes and not exclusively with stylized Nature. The period of assimilation and adjustment is bound to be as long as in poetry, if not longer.

When and what the Japanese understand, they understand so perfectly, so sensitively and, it seems, instinctively. It is very probable that the craze for 'foreign' art has led to a lowering of standards in the national art of ceramics, outside of the work of Kawai Kanjirō and a few other masters.   One's first impulse is to deplore this—a birthright has been sold for a mess of pottage.   Yet one ought to bear in mind the narrow emotional range and the limited themes of the traditional Japanese arts when compared with the arts of Europe.   It seems to be another of those sacrifices that have to be made— a temporary 'thinning' which cannot be helped if Japanese aesthetic understanding is to *expand*.

THE JAPANESE HOUSE

I am thinking of the Japanese House as eulogized by foreign connoisseurs and as exported to foreign countries for exhibition.   Simplicity and taste, a refined bareness, a serene and spiritual atmosphere, and the best of materials.   Yes, but where are these famous houses ?

The truth is that the traditional type of Japanese house is a very fine creation on its highest levels, when built for men of considerable taste and wealth.   But even on the level of the middle-class income, the Japanese house tends oddly in the direction of what we should describe as a slum.   That is to say, it is either very impressive or else it is in some degree dingy, uncomfortable and over-crowded.   A small Japanese house, with its *tatami* and *shōji* (sliding screens of wood and paper used as walls), offers more possibilities for squalor than a correspondingly small foreign-style house, particularly if there are children (which there usually are, in abundance). Even in a large and rich house, however exquisite its taste, there appears to be no traditional and convenient provision for books : for that item you need a 'foreign-style' parlour— a phenomenon which foreigners of taste have always ridiculed ('foreign-style ?—yes, foreign to all known styles ! '). If the Japanese intellectual has a foreign-style room it is not aping of the west— it is a practical measure designed to give him somewhere to work efficiently.

Moreover, the constant struggle against dust—that prime enemy of *tatami*—is apt to lead to insufficient ventilation and the continuous and indiscriminate throwing about of water. It also involves considerable domestic labour—in fact, like the kimono, *tatami* is beautiful but not wholly suited to democracy. The Japanese have never, traditionally, thought of the house as a machine for living—they have thought of it as a work of art. But alas, the human body—like the human spirit—is only a work of nature.

What I have said refers to the Japanese house on its higher levels of achievement. There are not so many, still in private hands, on those levels today. In its average form, the Japanese house is dimly lighted, hot in summer and cold in winter, quickly cluttered up with magazines, papers, reading lamps and trunks. On its lowest level, it is merely a shack. *Tatami*, however reverentially treated, is not hard-wearing; it really needs to be replaced every two or three years [1]—and few people can afford to do that. Nothing looks more slummy than *tatami* which has worn through in places. Today most of the houses being built use wooden floorboards for the living rooms, with *tatami* reserved for the sleeping-rooms (one cannot call them 'bedrooms' as beds are uncommon) and perhaps for a guest-room. Both financial and practical considerations are bringing about this sensible departure from copy-book traditionalism.

My remarks are not intended in a spirit of malice. If the 'Japanese house' were actually as the romantics have supposed and desired, then the Japanese really would be the devotees of Cult, of Form, of Preciosity which so many westerners complain that they are. Furthermore, can the Japanese expect the British to respond sympathetically to their complaints of poverty and their need for increased trade if the Lancashire textile workers are left under the impression that

[1] There is a proverb which says, 'As for *tatami* and wives, the newer the better.' Out of fairness to faithful Japanese husbands we must add that there is another proverb: 'As for kettles and wives, the older the better.'

a sizeable proportion of the Japanese people live in elegant and artistic structures whose light-weight materials are due solely to the danger of earthquakes? The Japanese must learn that they cannot be fabulous and destitute at the same time—at least not before the bar of world opinion. Though the average modern Japanese house of the middle-class type is often an unhappy mixture of Japanese and foreign in which the former elements are debased and the latter ill-made and misapplied, at least I have been relieved to see that the inhabitants are real people, with normal interests, not hopelessly subordinated to any deathly cult of Form.

Still, a curious vestige of repression lingers on. Japanese joiners can make fine *shōji* and other such accessories–but their attempts at hanging a simple door and fitting it with a handle that really works are pathetic. Why? One cannot believe that they are honestly incapable of such elementary jobs—Japanese workmen show remarkable ingenuity and intelligence elsewhere. No, one is forced to the conclusion that they still, in their innermost hearts, despise foreign appurtenances; and that they despise them even though they employ them, to their greater comfort, in their own homes. This ambivalent attitude is the most disquieting thing about Japan : the unconscious feeling that the old native discomfort is somehow morally superior to the new foreign comfort. It exists in the political world, in the field of government, and it operates as an unseen drag on the putting into practice of social reforms.

The irony of it is that well-meaning foreigners, with all the right and creditable ideas about social reform, are busily encouraging the Japanese in all sorts of artistic and even social habits which are incompatible with that social reform. The western democracies, it seems, still have their repressed dreams of impossible feudal beauties and ancient quaintnesses -dreams which they look to Japan to bring to life, at whatever expense to the poor Japanese. Democracy—I could not define the word myself, but I am convinced that what Japan must somehow achieve is a greater respect for the individual as an individual, not as a featureless member of a certain social class or profession, but as an individual in his or her own right.   I was once a guest at a business dinner in a celebrated Kyoto *chaya* where geisha were in attendance.   There were twelve of us and the cost came to £10 per head.   Reading afterwards how a fifteen-year-old girl had been sold into prostitution for £2 (an exceptionally modest price : it had been a bad year for farmers), it struck me that at this rate we had each consumed part of the youth of five girls at that dinner, or sixty between us.   This would seem to be a fairly clear example of what democracy at least is *not*.   Life is continuous : you cannot make changes at one point without affecting it all along the line.   In fact, you cannot have your cake and eat it—a delusion to which the Japanese are prone enough without help and encouragement from outside. It is significant that America, the most determined and assured exponent of the rights of man, should come to Japan to pick forbidden fruit more enthusiastically and energetically and more naïvely than anyone else.

Japanese architecture has suddenly attained great popularity in America.   Popular magazines, we gather, print articles informing their readers how they may incorporate typical Japanese motifs into their houses.   The professor of architecture in a large American university is quoted as having said that, ' In contrast to American architecture which is an outcrop of mechanized civilization, that of Japan is born of Mother Nature and built from materials grown of the Good Earth.' If by Japanese architecture we mean the average Japanese house, then true enough, it is built from materials grown of the Good Earth—sand and straw and water used generously and cement used sparingly ; or wood which left the breast of Mother Nature so long ago that it is more corpse-like than anything which man could make.   As for ' mechanized civilization ', that is an old term of abuse ; and with the population of this small and mountainous country estimated to reach a hundred million in about twenty years' time, it is clear that its civilization must be either ' mechanized ' or non-

existent.   Such ignorant romancing is worse than silly ; it is
dangerous.   The Japanese are in an uneasy transitional stage :
they are particularly susceptible to foreign opinion when it
flatters their past—and such thoughtless eulogies as these
provide a tug in the wrong direction.   The professor should
come to Japan and take a look at the houses in which the
majority of Japanese live—small, over-crowded, insanitary,
lacking in any privacy, and liable to collapse during the yearly
typhoon season.[1]   He would rush back thankfully to his
'outcrop of mechanized civilization' with its solid walls, its
taps that actually turn on and off, its large windows, its tactful
sanitation and its central heating.   Thank heavens the Japanese are more sensible than their foreign devotees : more and
more blocks of flats are going up, healthy-looking stoves are
pushing out the little *hibachi* or charcoal brazier ('that ghost of
a fire', as even Lafcadio Hearn confessed),[2] and sometimes
there is a playground for the children of the block so that they
don't have to play on the traffic-crowded streets or about the
railway tracks.   How unromantic it all is.

Of course, the old Japanese house is a beautiful object.
Every visitor to Japan visits the Katsura Detached Palace in
Kyoto—and so he should.   It is the apotheosis of what for us
is the difficult art of simplicity.   It is a show-place.   That is my
point.   Only a work of art can live comfortably in a show-place.

Perhaps the real subject of this book is the struggle in which
the Japanese are at present involved, to liberate themselves

---

[1] Figures lie, they say—but not as grossly as the artistic souls
and the tourist brochures.   The figures say that in Tokyo there are
1,210,000 houses, of which two per cent are ferro-concrete build-
ings.   The remainder are what the *Asahi Evening News* describes
as 'the usual "wood-and-paper" flammable houses'.

[2] Hearn freezing in his house differed from Hearn writing about
'The Genius of Japanese Civilization'—cf. 'Nature has given
him (the Japanese) . . . a constitution that scorns heat, cold, and
damp alike, because still unimpaired by unhealthy clothing, by
superfluous comforts, by the habit of seeking warmth from grates
and stoves, and by the habit of wearing leather shoes' (*Kokoro*).

from the bonds of ' Tradition ', from the anti-human stylization of the old ' Japanese Spirit '.   Living in Japan has made
me increasingly sceptical about ' Tradition ', that god to
which we in the west pay lip service, if nothing more.   Japan
is *the* country of Tradition, and thus fair game for any sentimental traveller and wealthy tourist who knows he hasn't got
to live in it.   One is reminded of the traditional *obi*, the wide
sash bound tightly round the kimono at breast level.   It is a
beautiful object, and its purpose seems to have been to conceal,
in the interests of femininity, one of the chief feminine characteristics.   This it has done so successfully through the ages
that modern Japanese girls, wearing a blouse or a jumper,
often have to turn to ' falsies ' to restore the balance.   ' Tradition ' has bound up the Japanese people, they have twisted
themselves into a strait-jacket more narrow than any lunatic
asylum could boast.   ' Tradition ' seems notably anti-human.
And if we wince at some of the current manifestations of
relaxation and ' westernization ', let us hope that they, like the
' falsies ', may prove only a stop-gap.

BUSHIDO : THE WAY OF THE WARRIOR

Bushido—the celebrated book by Dr. Inazō Nitobe—was
published first in 1899 with the subtitle, ' The Soul of Japan '.
Basil Hall Chamberlain, as sceptical but as sensible as ever,
remarks that the word ' bushido ' appears in no dictionary,
native or foreign, before the year 1900.   But Dr. Nitobe's
book had an immense success ; sponsored by foreign Christians in Japan (he was a Christian himself), it was translated
into every major language and several minor ones.   In a
recent BBC talk, Dr. Gilbert Murray referred to the theory in
a tone of some respect ; and the C.O.D. defines the word as
' the code of honour and morals evolved by the samurai '.
Perhaps the definition should rather read, ' evolved by a
scholarly and patriotic Christian Japanese gentleman, propa-
gated by foreign missionaries and romantics, and exploited
by native militarists ; now apparently obsolete '.
    Let us look briefly at what exactly it was that so excited

these well-intentioned Christians.   The first obstacle would seem to lie in the fact that the samurai's loyalty unto death is due to his lord and not to God.   And in fact Dr. Nitobe, in defending Japanese Christians against the accusation of dis-loyalty to the Throne brought against them by ' the misguided (Japanese) disciples of Spencer ', quotes the very text itself, ' Render unto Caesar . . .'   Christian countries have solved similar dilemmas in a similar way, to their own satisfaction.

The way of the warrior was considerably more repressive than that of any Christian sect ; and its training began at an early age : ' Does a little booby cry for any ache ?   The mother scolds him in this fashion : " What a coward to cry for a trifling pain !   What will you do when your arm is cut off in battle ?   What when you are called upon to commit *hara-kiri* ? " '   (That sends one back to Freud with a new respect !)   A favourite pastime of the sons of samurai, Dr. Nitobe tells us, was to go on pilgrimages to graveyards and haunted houses, and ' in the days when decapitation was public, not only were small boys sent to witness the ghastly scene, but they were made to visit alone the place in the dark-ness of night and there to leave a mark of their visit on the trunkless head '.

Bushido, as Dr. Nitobe expounds it, is rich in literature, rich in striking sayings and stirring stories.   He tells of the young son of Ieyasu who was forcibly confined to the rear of the army during his father's siege of Osaka.   Finding him in tears, an old councillor reminded the boy that he would have plenty of opportunities in the future to distinguish himself. ' How foolishly you talk !' replied the boy indignantly, ' Can ever my fourteenth year come round again ? '   A good example of the Japanese version of the Shropshire Lad.

Rich in literature, yes, but notably poor in life.   It is, in truth, a conception essentially anti-human and ' artistic '. Where life was concerned, this was its attitude : ' I know of a father who spent whole nights listening to the breathing of a sick child, standing behind the door that he might not be caught in such an act of parental weakness ! '

More interesting from the point of view of the present book is Dr. Nitobe's insistence on the importance of forms. The tea ceremony, *cha no yu*, is simply table manners elevated to ritual. But, Dr. Nitobe asks, ' Is lofty spiritual attainment really possible through etiquette ? Why not ?—All roads lead to Rome ! ' Developments which Dr. Nitobe was spared from witnessing go to suggest that, on the contrary, the only thing that etiquette leads to is etiquette. When etiquette is as rigid and prescribed as that which he describes (or which Kakuzō Okakura hints at in words which once captured the imagination of the west, ' Our etiquette begins with learning how to offer a fan, and ends with the rites for committing suicide '), it means that, when the individual is faced by an unusual situation, he tends to break down. Will the knowledge of how he would be expected to behave under different circumstances prevent him from behaving in an unfortunate manner now ? All roads may lead to Rome— but in an emergency one needs to take a short-cut, and reliance upon oneself is the only available one.

Self-reliance is a virtue which the Japanese have traditionally discouraged (a fact that should endear them to our own inveterate medievalists)—it could lead to ' unexpected ' behaviour. That is perhaps why, even today, there are so many literary scholars to so few literary critics. And that is perhaps why, once etiquette has been relaxed, the members of the Diet are liable to fling themselves upon each other tooth and nail. But the man in the street is learning to rely upon himself—he is finding out that in this changing world only thus can he hope to survive. Let us pray that he may survive even his politicians—and his foreign counsellors.

After the noble stories of self-sacrifice and all the rest of this literature of death, what is left in Dr. Nitobe's Bushido, at the heart of it ? The heart of it is as misty as ever—Dr. Nitobe, that good Christian, passes the buck : ' A foremost teacher of swordsmanship, when he saw his pupil master the utmost of his art, told him, " Beyond this my instruction must give way to Zen teaching." '

It must be added that Dr. Nitobe's life was more logical than his writing. He was an influence for good in the Japan of his time, and his work for the League of Nations gained international respect for his country. The son of a samurai family himself, converted to Christianity in his sixteenth year, we can understand his attempts to reconcile the two ' codes '. It is less easy to sympathize with the assumption of his foreign Christian admirers that he had succeeded—or even that he had revealed an antique code of morals worthy of that name.

Yukichi Fukuzawa, that indefatigable nineteenth-century exponent of the ways of the west, once said, ' Religion is like tea. You choose the tea whose flavour you like best, and you buy from the tea-merchant who sells it.' Basil Hall Chamberlain repeats a common foreign opinion when he writes, ' People will never greatly excite themselves about beliefs that sit lightly on them ; and Japanese religious beliefs have always sat lightly.' And, for we should quote a contemporary Japanese opinion, Rintarō Fukuhara adds, ' Shintoism no less than Buddhism is, at least for me and for a great number of us, a ritual necessary to give some picturesque finishing touch to certain events in our home or community life.' [1] Yet it is not exactly what we call ' sincerity ' that is lacking, if by that we mean the readiness to die for an adopted attitude. It is rather that Japanese religious thinking strikes us as ' amorphous '—a commitment to something which we would consider an exclusive line of belief apparently does not exclude a certain care for other and (as we should consider) incompatible lines of belief. Perhaps the Japanese have remained closer to their primitive *kami*—the swarming gods, both national and local, which early documents number at ' eight hundred myriad '—and have been less inclined to hunt for heresy. Perhaps they found relief from the rigid structure of the family and the state in the vast cobweb of religious

[1] ' Women, Gods and Letters ', *Japan Quarterly*, Vol. I, No. 1, October–December 1954, Tokyo.

possibilities. You had one liege lord, but you could have many gods.

Certainly the persecution of Christians in Japan had nothing of the Inquisition's zeal for Truth about it : Christianity was officially banned because the missionaries were suspected to be the forerunners of an invading army and Japanese Christians therefore a potential Fifth Column. It was foreign flags that the Tokugawa shoguns objected to, and not religious banners : with eight million native gods in the country, not to mention popular spirits and demons, a few foreign deities could easily be assimilated, and could even be equally true. The account which Sir George Sansom gives of the oaths which apostates from Christianity were compelled to swear after 1616 is both amusing and instructive :

In denying the Christian faith each apostate had to repeat reasons for his disbelief in a prescribed formula, which ran : ' The Fathers, by threat of excommunication and hell fire, can do what they like with the people, *and all this is their stratagem to take the countries of others.*' The remainder of the formula is an involuntary tribute to the power of the Christian faith, for the converts, having abjured their religion (generally under duress), were by a curious logic made to swear by the very powers that they had just denied : ' By the Father, the Son and the Holy Ghost, Santa Maria and all the Angels . . . if I break this oath may I lose the Grace of God forever and fall into the wretched state of Judas Iscariot.' By an even further departure from logic all this was followed by an oath to Buddhist and Shinto deities.

Foreign residents in Japan, and particularly business men, tend to speak rather derogatorily about Japanese Christians : western clothes are now commonly accepted, so one does not distrust a Japanese employee who wears them—but a Japanese employee who sports a Christian name. . . . A second implication is that the Japanese Christian, unlike the European or American business man, probably doesn't understand Christianity properly. . . . Support for this theory might be found in Captain John Saris's story of his arrival in Japan in 1613. In his cabin he had a picture of Venus and Cupid

which he described as ' somewhat wantonly set out '. Some
of the Japanese Christian women who visited the boat, ' thinking it to be our Lady and her Son, fell down and worshipped
it, with shows of great devotion '. A laughable tale, no doubt.
But we should also take notice of another incident related by
the same visitor. Twenty-seven Japanese Christians who
had celebrated mass within the proscribed area of Edo (Tokyo)
were shut up in a cell overnight. A non-Christian Japanese,
guilty of nothing more heinous than debt, was later thrown in
among them. The next morning those who would not
renounce Christianity were called out to execution. The
debtor, converted during the night, walked out with them and
was crucified. There is no question about the courage and
resolution with which a Japanese will follow his leader once
he has chosen him. The disquietening point is how he arrives
at his choice. The man in this story could perhaps not have
' learnt ' much about Christianity in the course of that one
night. . . .

I have personally never heard the word ' Bushido ' on the
lips of a Japanese, except when Dr. Nitobe was under discussion; and I have heard Japanese criticizing Dr. Nitobe
for his dubious logic. It would be nice to know for sure that
Bushido had received its *coup de grâce*—lest some resurgent
Right Wing extremist party should be tempted to revivify
this myth.

LAFCADIO HEARN

It may be as well to remind the western reader that Lafcadio
Hearn was the son of an Irish father and a Greek mother, that
he worked as a newspaperman in the Middle West, travelled
in the tropics, and finally arrived in Japan in 1890. Here he
was given a teaching post in a remote provincial town, was
later promoted to the Imperial University of Tokyo, married
a Japanese lady, took Japanese nationality, and wrote many
books about old Japan. Basil Hall Chamberlain, who knew
him personally, tells us that the Japanese government was

disappointed in Hearn, ' for it had engaged him convinced that he would bring European public opinion to favour all the modern changes which, on the contrary, he never ceased to curse '. But the wheel has come full circle, and now Lafcadio Hearn is (almost) a national hero in Japan. His opinions on the land of his adoption are continually being quoted in the Japanese press (particularly that section of it catering for foreigners) ; every foreign visitor is hastily lent his books ; his works form favourite recitation pieces in school contests, and only too frequently feature as set texts in the universities. (I had better confess before going any further that I have turned out a sore disappointment to some of my sponsors by failing, as this book sufficiently indicates, to rise to the role of the Second Lafcadio Hearn for which I was cast in advance.) I am pretty sure that somewhere or other could be found a Bar Lafcadio or a Hotel Hearn.

It is easy to understand why the Japanese, at this sensitive moment in their history, should find consolation not merely in a foreign writer who devoted himself to Japan but in one who, the moment he had landed, wrote off enthusiastically about the divinity of the race, crying, ' *We* are the barbarians ! ' Too many of the older people, particularly those in comfortable circumstances, prefer his literary conception of the Old Japan to the present ambiguities of the Real Japan, I suspect. But what is less easy to comprehend is that university professors of eminence have throughout taught their students to believe that Lafcadio Hearn is a classic of English (American ?) literature. And even stranger, no foreigner who has taught literature in the country has—to my knowledge—made any protest against this large assumption. (If the sensitive reader feels that my remarks are in bad taste, he can console himself that no one is likely to take them seriously.)

The truth is that Hearn, in both his life and his writings, was a typical and thorough-going specimen of *fin de siècle* romanticism. His speciality was ' the exotic ', and he sought for it desperately ; if he could not find it in the present, then he was tempted to fabricate it in the past, even at the cost of

denigrating the present reality. A letter which he wrote
from New Orleans in 1883 contains a significant admission :
' Knowing that I have nothing resembling genius, and that
any ordinary talent must be supplemented with some sort of
curious study in order to place it above the mediocre line,
I am striving to woo the Muse of the Odd, and hope to succeed
in thus attracting some little attention . . .'

New Orleans palled on him and Martinique finally let him
down. Japan, a little-known country, offered a richer field.
Perhaps it was as a kind of insurance policy against future
disillusionment that he took a Japanese wife, for he knew that
he must then settle in Japan for the rest of his days. He had
burnt his boats.

The Hearn myth strikes me as dangerous because it
is the classic, the most powerful, instance of the foreign
devotee praising a past in which he would never have had
to live and complaining bitterly of those inevitably crude
efforts which the people were at last making to loosen the
traditional social chains. A few quotations from his letters
will suffice :

I gave seventy-two boys, as subject for composition the other
day, the question : ' What would you most like in this world ? '
Nine of the compositions contained in substance this answer :
' To die for our Sacred Emperor '. That is Shintō. Isn't it
grand and beautiful ? and do you wonder that I love it after that ?

Presumably he gave those boys full marks, and the others
soon saw the light : they themselves would have been too old
to become *kamikaze* pilots. A statement in *Kokoro : Hints
and Echoes of Japanese Inner Life* indicates the perversity of
his enthusiasm, and will perhaps suggest why I feel it worth
while to flog what to western readers must seem a very dead
horse—he still kicks in the east :

We are accustomed to think that some degree of stability is
necessary to all real progress, and great development. But
Japan has given proof irrefutable that enormous development is

possible without any stability at all. The explanation is in the race character . . .

It was to another acquaintance that he wrote this :

The Japanese of the new school . . . are becoming infected with the Western moral poison. They are beginning to love their wives more than their fathers and mothers. . . .

He became *plus japonais que le Japon*—but did he become Japanese ? When he took Japanese nationality the government, with a flash of devastating logic, cut his salary from the foreign to the native grade, and he wrote complainingly to an American friend that ' the Japanese Government . . . told me that I ought to be satisfied to live on rice, like a Japanese '.

Hearn—as all of us must do—fell for the Japanese woman :

But how sweet the Japanese woman is !—all the possibilities of the race for goodness seem to be concentrated in her. It shakes one's faith in some Occidental doctrines. If this be the result of suppression and oppression—then these are not altogether bad.

Is it this mixture of vague evocativeness, sentimentality and curious illogic which has helped to endear him to the older Japanese intellectuals ? The point is that under ' suppression and oppression ' the possibilities for goodness of which he speaks cannot be realized ; they exist behind a glass case, in the ' inner room ' ; they remain as ' womanish things ', enjoyed in the body and perhaps admired in the heart, but despised in the mind. ' Power corrupts '—it may do ; but the spiritual powerlessness of the women whom he praises was also a kind of corruption—a corruption of the Japanese male.[1]

[1] In spite of the *senryū* which Mr. Blyth translates thus :
' We women . . . ! '
A skinny creature
Stands there
—Japanese feminists seem rather mild by western standards. Judging from their occasional pronouncements in the press, the country's distaff intellectuals appear to feel that while in Japan the male is treated with excessive concern, in America the female is definitely spoilt.

11. Kiyomizu Temple, West Gate, Kyoto.

12. Gion Festival, Kyoto.

The human virtues were separated into watertight compartments : the samurai's wife was the embodiment of mildness,
and so the samurai himself, once outside the family circle, was
to embody courage—divorced from mildness. But Hearn
did not stop to ask himself why he could not get very close
to the men, why (as he put it in another letter) ' one's best
friends have a certain far-offness about them, even when
breaking their necks to please you ! '

Even so, Hearn's motives were pure. It is less easy to
forgive the latter-day romanticism of an apparently hard-
boiled newspaper-woman who writes thus of the Japanese, in
1949 : ' Their social ways seemed better in so many respects
than those of Europe. But for many years this delicate civilization had been exposed to the bruising impact of the west :
and now, the west, having overwhelmed it physically, was
concerned to destroy, if it could, the spirit which had given it
birth ' [1]—when the rest of her book shows that she is only
praising old Japan (which was certainly not the fragile flower
she implies) in order to blacken new America. It is the same
newspaper-woman who complains thus : ' If you admire the
kimono a woman is wearing, she immediately tells you how
awkward it is in trains.' Who knows best—Miss Tracy or
the woman who has worn a kimono on and off (for instance,
to meet foreign visitors in) ever since she was born ? Or
does Miss Tracy propose to abolish the trains ? Or perhaps
confine women—I mean Japanese women, of course—to the
home ?

Hearn's best books, I think, are the collections of weird
stories—that was where his talent lay, and where ' the Muse
of the Odd ' could best disport herself honestly—and his
serious-minded study, *Japan : An Interpretation*. It is true
that in the latter he talks of the ' religious quality ' in the old
Japanese stories of revenge and describes the famous tale of
the Forty-seven Rōnin as ' a romance of loyalty '—whereas
it is also a noxious section of that crimson thread which has
run through Japanese life right up to today : the stifling of

[1] *Kakemono*, by Honor Tracy, London, 1950.

L

normal affections and the shocking wastage of human lives. But the book is free from that embarrassing pseudo-mystical gush which floods his more 'sensitive' essays (for example, on the Japanese Smile : an essay which would be sufficient by itself to account for the modern *sensei's* resolution never to smile again), and he even goes so far as to admit that 'the sense of individual moral responsibility has not yet been sufficiently cultivated outside of the group-relation'.

It is pleasant to be able to say that the final words on Lafcadio Hearn were spoken by a Japanese—by his wife. After his death she wrote to his biographer in this wise : 'He put too much importance to Beauty or Nicety perhaps. . . . Indeed sometimes I thought he was mad, because he seemed too frequently he saw things that were not and heard things that were not.'

No one seems to have paid much attention to what she said. But that is the true voice of the patient and realistic Japanese woman, whenever she is asked to raise it. I hope that we may hear it more often.

11 : JAPAN FOR EXPORT

> ' The dead are gone and with them we cannot converse.
> The living are here and ought to have our love . . .'
>   (*Old Chinese poem, trans. Arthur Waley*)

UNLIKE the French *chanson*, things American are not particularly fashionable in Japan at present, since the H-bomb
test and the consequent death of one of the seamen. In
America, however, it seems that things Japanese are definitely
chic—Stratford-on-Avon will have to look to its laurels.

International relations would no doubt be more honest
were there fewer of them. Today's hero is apt to be tomorrow's villain ; and of course *vice versa*. Once you have
knocked down your enemy, you have to pick him up quickly
and stop his nose bleeding—for you can never rely on your
friends for long. . . . It is amusing but saddening to watch
the way in which cultural relations ebb and flow in time with
the great erratic waves of power politics.[1]

U.S. personnel stationed in the country have been a boon

---

[1] If the Americans might seem to have poured out their sudden
love for Japan with undignified haste, the British have erred in the
opposite direction. A girl student was telling me of her ambition
to go to England for further study. ' But,' she added sadly, ' I am
told that the English do not like the Japanese people.' ' Oh,' I
assured her, ' you needn't worry about that at all ! ' But then, she
was very pretty.

No one would suggest that Britain should fall upon Japan's
neck ; but we could show more interest in her position and more
understanding of her pressing problems. It is not our implaca-
bility, but our lack of knowledge (except on one or two painful
points) and perhaps the fact of distance, which these days is an
illusion.

to the souvenir trade (dragons, Fuji and temples), but some of
them have spent their money well. After all a cigarette
lighter may actually work even though decorated with a
geisha girl in technicolour. It is the more ambitious type of
tourist who propounds the puzzle—the one who is not content
with prints, *kakemono*, pottery and lacquer work alone, but
insists on taking a Japanese cult home with him. Even in
their native surroundings where they have been practised for
centuries, some of these cults are wearing thin. How they
look under the breezier skies of the New World defies
imagination.

I am not thinking of *ikebana*, Flower Arrangement, a
favourite pastime among the wives of foreign residents. For
women, being more sensible than men, are usually content to
achieve an attractive result and thus avoid losing themselves
in the clouds of the accompanying mystique. The language
of flowers, after all, is reasonably international.[1]

Cha no yu is the latest applicant for American nationality ;
and here, however, one feels less happy. The International
Association for the Advancement of the Japanese Tea Cult
(as it calls itself) has published a small book in English which
confirms one's worst fears. It begins with the unfortunate
statement that ' There is nothing but the tea ceremony to make
Japanese keep the morals, educate their character in order to
advance their daily living.' The relevance of this to Dr.
Nitobe's remarks about the spiritual value of etiquette is
obvious. The Association's statement is not true, happy to
say : but it is something which the Japanese have told themselves so often in the past that they almost came to believe it.

---

[1] Whenever my wife puts a few flowers in a vase our visitors—
Japanese and also foreigners who take lessons in *ikebana*—invariably ask her who her flower arrangement *sensei* is. This assumption that natural taste doesn't really exist and that everything must
be done through ' instruction ' seems to me rather Japanese. A
similar assumption—except that it holds that everything *can* be
done through instruction—appears to underlie the present university education system.

And that—if I may repeat myself—is perhaps why the Diet, finding that politics is no tea ceremony, too easily declines into something like feeding-time at the Zoo.

The early Zen Buddhists used tea for the eminently practical reason of warding off drowsiness while at their meditations. Possibly they enjoyed it, too—but enjoyment is a low vulgar thing which no person of taste or profundity would associate himself with for a moment. Being thus connected with Zen, the practice of tea-drinking came to assume some of the characteristics of a religious rite. But during the fifteenth century, according to the same book, Tea Ceremony ' was fully constituted and made into an independent and secular performance '. Unlike the English drama, however, it preserved a good deal of the aura of a religious exercise. Its position in the Japanese traditional arts is undoubtedly important, for it influenced both potters (through the utensils used) and garden architects (through the garden which is a necessary part of the decor). But it has to be admitted, I think, that its influence has also been to widen that gulf between life and art which we have noticed elsewhere, for its aim has been to provide a standardized Ivory Tower—an oasis of peace in the midst of the stormy life led by the warrior or the man of business. It has always set out deliberately to create a special set of conditions opposed in every particular to those obtaining outside the tea-room. For instance, in a strictly caste society, the tea ceremony was democratic : the samurai had to leave his swords in a special hanger outside the tea-room, and the entrance to the room was and is always small and low so that everyone must humble himself at the outset. Similarly, while the street outside is likely to be dirty, the tea-room will be immaculate, and if a dead leaf should be seen lying on the path of the garden, you can be sure that someone has placed it there in the interests of art.

' The devotees,' the book continues, ' are enabled to promote friendship among themselves in a congenial and aesthetic atmosphere which is conducive to restfulness, simplicity, courtesy and urbanity.' And Mr. Sōko Sen, head of the tea-school promulgating this book, in a recent (July 1954) issue of the magazine *Geijutsu Shinchō* (' Art's New Tide '), com-pared his *cha no yu* cultural system with Moral Rearmament and claimed that the principle of harmony-respect-quiet-serenity which tea masters spread is ' deeper ' than MRA as a peace doctrine. These aims are worthy enough. But considering the extreme deliberation of the whole ceremony —it takes four hours, including the preparatory waiting, the ritual washing, the admiring of the *kakemono*, the meal, the withdrawal of the guests and their re-entry, the serving of the Tea and the admiring of the utensils—it seems a curiously self-conscious method of achieving these results. Again, one wonders whether the impeccable restfulness of the tea-room is not connected in some way with the awful and un-disciplined din outside. Mutually exclusive categories are inclined to exacerbate each other. Art and life, in this way of looking at them, are more remote from each other than we in the west have ever believed. That was a consideration brought home to me very painfully while walking in the garden of the Ura-Senke School of tea ceremony in Kyoto, in the garden in which one's spirit attains ' a perfect impersonal beatitude, far from the hustle and bustle of life '. I was savagely bitten by some peculiarly unaesthetic mosquitoes.

The full tea ceremony is rather a strain for those foreigners unused to kneeling on *tatami* and to slowness and long periods of silence (witty conversation is not encouraged). And when the Japanese specialists seek to make the performance shorter and easier, they are honestly endeavouring to please, and there is no sycophancy in it. The obloquy attaches to the foreigner who supposes that a ' modified ' and truncated ceremony can be packed into his bag and taken back home for the future edification of his soul and his neighbours. But the tea cere-mony master has already softened him up by a clever appeal to both sides of his western nature—firstly by quoting the rather picturesque Ten Virtues of Tea as propounded by the monk Myō-e Shōnin (' Has the blessing of all the deities ', ' Promotes filial piety ', ' Destroys the passions ', ' Gives a peaceful death ', etc.), and secondly by assuring him that ' according to research recently conducted by specialists, who analysed various kinds of tea, Japanese green tea, of which the best leaves are powdered, contains a considerable quantity of Vitamin C. It is interesting to note that Chinese green tea contains very little of Vitamin C, while there is no trace of it in the black tea produced in India and China.' The foreigner will now be less likely to raise any objection or be aware of suffering any humiliation when instructed in ' Simplified Ceremonial Tea ' (' held at offices, schools, or picnics in new Japan ') and ' Modernized Tea Ceremonial ', where tables and chairs are employed.

Tea ceremony, one suspects, is one of those things which either exist in their entirety or cease to exist at all. And those modified versions (for use in a fine American drawing room which may even be endowed with a carpet reminiscent of *tatami*, as a Japanese tea master told me on his return from opening branch schools in the U.S.) reminds me rather of how Poetic Drama in England today has been brought back on to the stage at the expense of quietly dropping the poetry.

The Japanese point of view seems paradoxical. Connoisseurs of tea ceremony are like all Japanese—so disarmingly pleased that foreigners should be interested in their national customs. But surely they cannot help but be torn between their pleasure in propagating their traditions and their respect for those traditions which they are simultaneously watering down. Their resultant state of mind, one would imagine, must be rather painful—unless they studiously refrain from thinking about the matter. I asked the tea master who had recently returned from America whether he thought that the ritual really went very deep there. He looked rather embarrassed and finally said, with a forgiving smile, ' Well, perhaps not very deep . . . at first . . .' One never knows—it might come to something : and so in the meanwhile the master (and perhaps his father could never have done this) continues to prosecute his cult on two levels, the domestic and the foreign, the real thing and the utility

model. And we have no right to put on superior airs—isn't
the principle of the literary digest accepted among us now?

The sad thing is that whereas all this slightly highbrow
'Madam Butterfly' business flourishes, the un-traditional arts
of Japan, the arts of the present, are practically unknown in
the west. The novel is certainly the most vigorous literary
form in Japan today: it has never been subject to rules and
regulations, and it has acquired no quasi-religious aura.
Admittedly one gathers that it has often taken advantage of
its freedom from things spiritual to over-indulge in things
physical. It may be that in the past the novelist, aware of his
exclusion from the magic circle of true art, did not bother to
take his functions seriously—just as the merchant in feudal
times, when trade was considered low and degrading, would
not strive to be less dishonest than he was expected to be.
But foreign examples—Gide, for example, who has had a great
vogue here—have vindicated the novel and made it respectable
in the eyes of the intellectuals as well as of the general public.
So we have every right to expect some truly responsible literature in this very influential form. It is good news that plans
are afoot for the translation into English of chosen works by
living novelists; and we trust that the choice will be left in
the hands of men of good taste as well as good will, and that
they will not be subject to the good intentions of the tourist
bureau mentality.

In July 1953 the U.S. Department of State issued an illustrated brochure under the title, ' Centennial Celebration of the
Opening of Japan '. It tells the story of the ' opening ' of
Japan by Commodore Perry, making some reference to
earlier Japanese history from 1542, when the first Europeans
(Portuguese traders) reached the country, up to 1868 and the
Meiji Restoration. The pamphlet ends with the assurance
that the United States and Japan ' know and understand each
other far better than we could in 1853 ', and with a pat on the
back for Japan for ' her generous and friendly gesture in sending to the U.S. a priceless collection of great Japanese art

treasures for showing in five American cities. These sculptures and paintings, dating from the sixth century A.D., are irreplaceable, but Japan is risking the hazards of weather and fire to let us see these masterpieces . . .'

Similar sentiments are expressed in the introductory note written by Mr. John Foster Dulles : ' As the first hundred years of our relations comes to a close, we can look forward to continued cordial relations of mutual advantage.' There is only one reference to the fairly recent Pacific War—a reference so indirect that the reader may well miss it altogether—and no allusion, however apt it would have been poetically, to the airborne ' black ships ' which Japan in her turn sent to Pearl Harbour. This is a notable error of tact : the Pacific War is terribly conspicuous by its absence.

The cat is let out of the bag (if indeed it could ever be said to have been in it) by the remark in the epilogue which contains the one indirect reference of which I spoke : ' A hundred years ago, Perry reported to Washington that one day a struggle for power between Russia and the Western world would take place at the rim of Asia. He urged fortification of the very islands of the far Pacific that we fortified in World War II and continue to fortify now. Today the U.S. and Japan face together the danger that Perry anticipated a hundred years ago.'

The situation is comprehensible enough : nearer home, the ' merchants of death ' have been relieved of the broad arrow and sent back to work. Even so, the simple naïvety of this document, the blatancy of its cupboard love which all the references to Japanese art treasures cannot conceal, its happy disregard of the merely human feelings on both sides ! It plays into the hands of the Japanese nationalist Right, who can claim that in ever distrusting the Russians and all ideas savouring of socialism they were just as far-sighted as Commodore Perry. As for the intelligentsia, the bugbear of the Rightists, the pamphlet is well calculated to confirm their fears that America is pushing them into a ' struggle for power at the rim of Asia ' for which they have not the slightest taste ; and on this point the man in the street—should he come across the pamphlet—will be at one with the intelligentsia.

Indeed, it is difficult to imagine what possible audience this celebratory pamphlet is aimed at and what possible good it can do. Even its interpretation of past history seems shaky, for its authors do not appear to realize that the so-called ' opening ' of Japan—popularly identified with the Meiji Restoration—coincided with the revival of the patriotic and anti-foreign Shinto which was declared the religion of State, and with the disendowment of the gentler Buddhism. That, in fact, the ' opening ' of Japan was a physical affair only, and that it was soon accompanied by a spiritual ' closing '. This dangerous situation exists still today—even in such harmless and insignificant matters as literature, the forms of the west are adopted while the spirit is lost in transit. The circumstances of the recent ' re-opening ' of Japan bear a sinister resemblance to those under which Perry secured his treaties : in each case the ' opening ' was effected by force and only because the Japanese military organization had proved incapable of keeping the foreigners out. The chief lesson which the Japanese learned on the first occasion was that their military organization should be improved. And the resultant feeling was that horrible one which ' John Paris ' describes in his novel, *Banzai !* (1925) : ' Thus, although foreigners were themselves inferior, yet everything which came from foreign countries was undoubtedly superior.'

We want no more of that disgusting state of affairs, in which the letter is divorced from the spirit and the technique split off from the human creature who uses it ; it is an open invitation to the H-bomb to eradicate a worthless species. One thing which Japan can do to help avoid it is to spare the west her humiliatingly ' simplified ' arty-crafty cults. And one thing the west can do is to spare Japan the mixture of simplified history and watered-down and ' adapted ' morals which passes as the expression of goodwill.

THE PIED PIPER OF AKASHI

A JAPANESE TALE

Despite the striking rows on rows of little stones,
      and large statistics,
Despite the vivid rags and ill-consorting bones—
      a fairy tale alone can make it real and true.

At ten in the morning the black planes flew
      across to bomb the factory
That made black planes.   A happy harmless time of day
For children and the aged, both at their various play.

The young ones and the old ones scurried to the park,
      the pretty refuge of the useless and the refuse
Of the race.   Away from the dark planes in the sky,
      the dark planes on the ground.

But in the morning brightness, the dazed planes found
A human target, by a human error, and let their sleeping
      brothers lie.
They taught the pines a lesson, the grass repented its
      aggression.   While nearby
The factory shuddered slightly at the sight.

That night the workers, back from perilous bench or office,
Found their home-town queerly run to middle age
      no docile daughters, no imps of sons,
And hardly any ancients, whether cracked or sage.

Yet time and our native riches have once again refuted
      the frozen spell of elves
And witches.   New old were soon recruited,
      from ourselves.

The young sprang up afresh, careless of wrongs and rights,
    to shame the frailer rice
And harass our economy.   They filled the ownerless kimonos,
    and flew their dusty brothers' kites.

The park is full of bold and bandy babies, and a glory
Of chrysanthemums and paper bags.   The nearby factory is
    full
Of busy adults, glittering planes, and foreign capital—
    a kindly fairy ends our little story.

12 : HAVING ONE'S CAKE AND EATING IT

> ' The bird in a forest can perch but on one bough,
> And this should be the wise man's pattern '
> *(Tso Ssŭ, trans. Arthur Waley)*

REPRESSION has its own peculiar beauties. So much good is mixed with so much that is indefensibly callous in traditional Japanese behaviour that today, when the unaesthetic concomitants of their transplanted democracy flourish so openly, it is understandable that many Japanese (and especially perhaps the more cultured) should look back to their past with nostalgia. Freedom they welcome sincerely, and yet they remember the glory that was feudal Japan. Whatever our nationality, few of us can avoid sentimentalizing the past.

Marilyn Monroe and Joe DiMaggio, both of them popular public figures, come to Japan. Crowds turn out to welcome the newly-weds ; the local papers print touching human stories about them ; someone, presumably her press agent, writes a life-history of Miss Monroe, to the effect that for all her curves she remains a nice simple ordinary American girl at heart. She announces that henceforward she will devote herself to making a home for Joe. Then, nine months later, the same papers print a shorter item to the effect that the two have decided to separate on account of the conflicting demands of their careers. So much, the Japanese observer may think, for equality of the sexes and careers for women and the nice simple ordinary heart of a female creature. He may call to mind the proverb, ' Never trust a woman, even if she has borne you seven children.' Or he may remember with nostalgia all those stories of self-sacrificing wives, before the west broke in—perhaps the story of Adzuma, who pretended to return the love which her husband's enemy professed for her, won his confidence, and lay down one night in her husband's place to receive the sword of her lover. And either way he may then echo the questions posed by the gentle Dr. Nitobe fifty-five years ago : ' Was not the loss of domesticity on the part of Roman matrons followed by moral corruption too gross to mention ? Can the American reformer assure us that a revolt of our daughters is the true course for their historical development to take ? '

Perhaps the very same Japanese who is working wholeheartedly for human rights and for the equality of women may at the same time take undue comfort from the gentle self-denial and submissiveness of his own wife. It is the same all over the world. The last lesson we learn is that we cannot really have our cake and actually eat it. It might be useful to refer the nostalgic to a passage in the *Tsurezure-Gusa* of Kenkō-hōshi, a Japanese recluse of the fourteenth century, whose ' writings to ward off tedium ' have for some reason appealed to so many foreign scholars. Kenkō is busy complaining that nothing in the present is nearly as good as it was in the past. The poetry of his day is utterly inferior to that of ' the ancients ' ; the contemporary head-dress is ridiculously high ; people's way of speaking has become shockingly vulgar. He reaches his great climax : today people do not even know the correct manner in which prisoners should be strapped to the flogging-frame—' It is said that nowadays there is nobody who understands the shape of this instrument, or the proper method of attachment.' [1]

I have already touched on a number of cases in which the Japanese contrive to eat their cake and still persuade themselves that it is safe in the cupboard. In 1889 private religious belief was declared to be free, but all Japanese were required to participate in State Shinto on top of the Buddhism or perhaps Christianity which they professed privately : this was

[1] Trans. G. B. Sansom, *Transactions of the Asiatic Society of Japan*, Vol. 39, 1911.

managed by declaring officially that State Shinto was not a religion but a separate subject which was to be taught in schools in the same spirit as history and geography were taught.   Today the sale of human beings is forbidden by law : but the geisha mistress can always ' adopt ' another daughter or two.   Similarly, bar-girls are not prostitutes and therefore are not required for medical examination as such : it is in their capacity as vendors of food and drink that they are obliged to carry a health certificate which happens to cover venereal disease.

There are many other modern instances.   Even in academic circles.   For example, the university lecture session of three hours (or even three and a half hours) duration, with a short break of ten minutes in the middle.   At first I took this seriously, with the result that I could not think or speak or even stand up for the rest of the day.   But I soon mastered the convention : the lecturer turns up some fifteen minutes late (he can be sure that his students will not disappear), he stretches out the break more or less *ad lib.*, and he finishes some fifteen minutes or so before time.   And that is common humanity, to all concerned—what I cannot understand is why the nominal schedule should be inhuman.   Moreover, to proceed to a doctorate in science it is necessary to publish five papers : a condition which is calculated, sensibly or otherwise, to render the degree difficult to obtain.   Since there are so many universities and, comparatively, so few independent scholarly journals, however, the condition is at once prohibitive. Hence every college publishes its own little research magazines (and in addition groups of teachers often print their own magazines at their own expense), so that the doctorate regulation loses its meaning entirely.

The Japanese public have always enjoyed ' love tragedies ' in fiction and on the stage, the same as anyone else.   But, in real life, to fall in love inappropriately was to commit a solecism, or rather a sin against the family unit : it was ' unexpected ' behaviour and no doubt retribution would follow. And so the implication was that no normal respectable woman

would get herself involved in a juicy ' love tragedy '—and
on the stage the heroine has generally been a geisha or prostitute of less fine feather, since such a person, being unrestrained,
was exactly the type to die for love.   In the orthodox Japanese
version of the tragedy, Romeo could certainly remain a well-
to-do and handsome young gentleman, but Juliet would have
to be stripped of her Capulet background and transformed
into a Veronese courtesan.   The rest of the story would
follow naturally : Montague could be the stern samurai
father, the shadowy Rosaline would be the wife chosen for
Romeo by his family, the Nurse would be Juliet's complaisant
double-dealing ' mamma san ' (' Now, by my maidenhead, at
twelve year old . . .'), and Paris her *dannasan* or ' protector '.
The double suicide, *shinjū*, would have to be quite deliberate,
and not fortuitous and morally shifty, as it is in Shakespeare ;
and then the play might be titled ' The Love Suicides in
Verona '.   Chikamatsu Monzaemon's play, *The Love Suicides
at Sonezaki* (1703), ends with the assuring words, ' they thus
became a model of true love '—something which the couple
could never have become by remaining alive.

A classical example in Europe of having one's cake and
eating it was the treatment accorded in the early Renaissance
to money-lenders.   These had been execrated as blasphemers
against God and Nature, but all the same towards the end of
the sixteenth century the old prohibition had to be relaxed
simply because the increasing opportunities in trade called for
fluid capital.   Usurers were hardly considered human, but
when their help was required, it was ' Shylock, we would have
moneys '.   Something of a comparable nature happened in
Japan with the rise of the pariah class called *eta*, the class
which provided executioners, butchers, leather-workers and
geta makers.   These occupations were considered unclean,
and yet somebody had to carry them out.

One theory has it that the *eta* are the descendants of Korean
captives brought to Japan during the later sixteenth century—
we saw a similar theory at work explaining away the modern
street-walkers—but Basil Hall Chamberlain suggests more

13. Fortune-teller.

14. *Geta* shop.

reasonably that their organization dates back to the seventh or eighth century when the introduction of Buddhism brought about a revulsion against those concerned with the taking of life (in which it seems human life was not included).   Like those other outcasts, the *Kabuki* actors, who purveyed the unclean commodity of pleasure, the *eta* used to be counted with the numerals proper to animals.   In an article in the magazine *Kaizō* (October 1954), Mr. Kiyoshi Inouye points out that the earlier *eta* were known as *kawara-mono*—that is, ' river-bed persons '—because their communities were located in unenviable positions, vulnerable to floods—while actors also were known by the same term.

The caste of *eta* was officially abolished as far back as 1871, when its members were given commoner status and termed *shin heimin* (' new commoners ') ; but the only advantage gained was the dubious one of liability to military conscription, which they had hitherto been denied.   The caste was officially re-abolished, of course, by the American-inspired ' New Constitution ' put into effect on 3 May 1947 (' there shall be no discrimination in political, economic, or social relations because of race, creed, sex, social status or family origin ').   But in effect it remains as well-defined as ever. Mr. Inouye states that in 1871, when the *eta* were given commoner status, they were afterwards told secretly by the village headmen that the decree was to take effect fifty thousand days later.   It was not necessary for them to be told anything the second time.   As in former years they lived in special districts on the outskirts of the towns and villages, so today they live in special districts inside the towns and villages. There are said to be six thousand such communities at the present time, with a total population of one and a half million. According to a member of the *eta* interviewed by Mr. Inouye, freedom of residence is still virtually unknown (which means that the *eta* districts have become the most densely populated of all) and the range of occupations open to them is still limited.

That the distinction exists quite firmly is indicated by the

M

fact that good-hearted Japanese are to be heard congratulating themselves that during the last war *eta* were satisfactorily drafted along with non-*eta*.   It is still rare, however, that a non-*eta* marries a husband or wife from among the *eta*.   The Japanese sometimes point out that the *eta* themselves are rather exclusive and show no great desire to mingle with the rest of the nation.   That there is no obvious discrimination against them may be connected with the fact that they carry out the discrimination themselves.   Some of them grow rich from their tanning and shoe-making but they will continue to live in the quarter, without making any show of their wealth. They have a reputation for miserliness.

A university professor once told me that he could always pick out an *eta* from among his students.   The interior of *eta* districts in the town is often distinguished by the smell of leather, but some Japanese claim to be able to tell just where a quarter begins.   I could never manage to find out how they did this, so it seems that they have a sixth sense—the sense of caste.   Once having recognized caste, they accept it fairly quietly on both sides : there are no outward signs of the snobbishness and the resentment which we know in the west. One should avoid thinking of these quarters as grim ghettoes or assuming sensationally that the *eta* have any history of persecution behind them comparable to that of the Jews in Europe.   The *eta* quarters in Kyoto are slum or near-slum districts, it is true—the air is dusty, the roads primitive, the houses are mostly shacks and the children ill-kept—but not all slum districts are *eta* quarters.

The *eta* who attempts (vainly) to escape from his class has featured as the hero of more than one work of fiction in the past (and Chamberlain mentions a Japanese adaptation of Wilkie Collins's *New Magdalen* in which the prostitute of the original is replaced by a girl who has degraded herself by marrying an *eta*).   But at least one modern political leader has come from that class.   In personal contact with them, the other Japanese show their usual courtesy ; and there is a politer appellation for them, characteristically enough—

Suihei-sha, 'water-level' or 'horizontal society' (i.e. very
equal).   Nonetheless, the *eta* exist and everyone is conscious
of the fact ; the conception of the moral equality of man has
made little headway on this point.   And I was aware of an
uncomfortable feeling, as of a bad conscience, in those Japanese with whom I talked on the subject.

The acceptance by the *eta* of their caste [1]—a phenomenon
which makes an early emancipation all the more unlikely—is
rather similar to the behaviour of Japanese madmen as reported
by an American psychologist in a recent book.[2]   He was
astonished to find that the most seriously deranged patients
were so docile that they could be confined in rooms with rice-
paper walls (*shōji*) and windows of thin glass.   The conclusion at which he arrived was that the traditions and institutions of the country were so strong that they could continue
to cow even the insane.   A Japanese friend who had visited
such asylums agreed that patients generally made no attempt
to escape, but said that he had observed them slowly and with
terrible deliberation tearing *tatami* into small pieces—which,
to Japanese ' traditional ' feeling, is an act amounting to
blasphemy.

Allied to having one's cake and eating it is the ability to
turn a blind eye.   We all have our moments of tactful blindness.   Perhaps it is the old tradition of ' not seeing until one
is expected to see ' (a piece of etiquette necessitated by the
small privacy afforded by Japanese houses) that enables the
Japanese to excel at this art.   To enjoy the cherry blossom
without noticing the cast out kitten starving slowly to death
beneath the tree—or to turn out for the respectable domestic
and tourist trade woodblock prints of a fine old Japanese house
which is still actually in use as a brothel.   In this hard world,
unfortunately, certain things occur which do not fit into the

[1] Which is not to say that anyone, Japanese or foreigner, would
be well advised to pronounce the word *eta* audibly in an *eta*
quarter.

[2] *Understanding the Japanese Mind*, by James Clark Moloney,
New York, 1954.

formal programme—these things are not exactly 'unexpected', but they are 'unremarked on'. Looking out one
day for a professor who was on his way to visit me and whom
I had not met previously, I thought I recognized my man and
I was about to hail him when he turned aside to look on the
hedge. I sped past, performed an about-turn, and slowly
approached him afresh. Such 'not noticing' is necessary
where private toilets are best spared and public ones hardly
exist. Blindness to wretched little kittens and puppies is less
easy to sympathize with.

As for Japanese traditions, I have mentioned more than
once my doubts as to whether some of the most charming and
irreproachable can still continue to survive in a truly democratic
country. The same Japanese who inveighs indignantly and
sincerely against all forms of the trade in flesh may yet praise
and seek in his own life to foster that extreme filial piety
which has led to such cruel self-sacrifice in the past and
which has helped to fill so many brothels. It is part of
traditional thought that a daughter should be prepared to sell
herself to a brothel-keeper in order to support her parents;
and while poverty still exists in Japan, 'filial piety' will continue to manifest itself in this way, and thus to ease temporarily
a situation which otherwise might demand and receive a more
radical and permanent cure. Too many people, one suspects,
do well out of 'filial piety'—though not the parents (who do
not get a very high price for their daughter as a rule), and not
the daughter (who has only the waning satisfaction of knowing that she has conformed to an ancient and noble tradition).

Yet the worst people for wanting to have their cake and eat
it are the cultured tourists from abroad, after all—together
with those foreign statesmen who want Japan to be peace-
abiding and militantly anti-Communist all at the same time.

13 : TWO INTERVIEWS

'Since I am convinced
That Reality is in no way
Real,
How am I to admit
That dreams are dreams?'
(*Saigyō Hōshi, trans. Arthur Waley*)

A BOOK, however short, which should fail to deal with the pressing concerns of the day—Japan's economic situation and her international position—would invite contempt, I fear. The present writer is totally unqualified to speak about such matters in the abstract terms considered proper to them—he is after all only a *sensei*—and he would have thought that sufficient attention had been paid to them elsewhere for him to be allowed to confine himself to the trivial matters of life : students and bars and poetry. However, advisers tell him otherwise. And perhaps—to look at it from a less worthy point of view for a moment—perhaps balance of payments really has a greater box-office appeal than geisha these days.

In the first of the following two interviews, questions and answers are printed in italics and comments by the author in roman type. I must admit that I seem to have done less than justice to the intelligence of the business man in question : I fear that I riled him slightly. But when he writes his book, then he shall have the last word.

THE BUSINESS MAN'S POINT OF VIEW

The Business Man in question is extremely clever and articulate, and very successful at his job ; he has had an academic training at a famous foreign university ; the firm of which he is president deals in general export and import.   In character he is a ' modern '.   ' Modern ' Japanese business men, following western principles, have sloughed most of the traditional ' paternalism ' towards their workers : and the onus of self-defence is therefore upon the workers, as has been the case in the west.   The clash between an ' old-fashioned ' employer's ' paternalism ' and his employees' more modern attitude (i.e. the organization of unions and the use of the strike weapon) has led to some odd emotional situations from which neither the resentful employer nor the letter-of-the-law union organizer emerges gracefully.   Obviously the two different systems cannot continue to exist side by side, and it seems right that, since ' paternalism ' cannot always be relied upon and may take strange shapes (as in the dispute referred to), it should yield to the colder modern forms of negotiation. A half-baked cake is good neither for having nor for eating. In the interim period, of course, there are a number of business men, both ' modern ' and ' old-fashioned ', who would like to dispense with both the personal and the public.

Q.   *What is the current Japanese attitude towards trade with Communist China?*

A.   *The majority of the public are in favour of it—and the majority of the business men.   Of course one's attitude varies according to one's political opinions . . . so many things do— including the eating of so-called radio-active fish.   The more anti-American or pro-Communist you are, the greater—and more vocal—your reluctance to eat H-bombed fish!*   (If you are pro-Communist you declare that Aikichi Kuboyama, the tuna fisherman who has just died after having been exposed to hydrogen radiation, was murdered by the Americans.   If you are pro-American then, like the Japanese Foreign Minister speaking in San Francisco, you hesitate to admit that Kubo-yama did actually die of hydrogen radiation.)   *First of all, the U.S.A. has lost some of its prestige recently :   that's one reason for the Japanese business men's attitude towards China. And then—this is an important point—many business men who are anti-Communist, of course, are also anti-Yoshida. And being anti-Yoshida, they are in favour of trade with China.* (He mentions the president of a large steel works who has lately had serious and protracted trouble with striking workers. This man slept for weeks in his office and was hardly seen by his family, such was the determination with which he fought to break the strike. Yet he is strongly in favour of increased trade with the Communists.) *Personally I am altogether opposed to trading with China—she has nothing to offer in return except what would profit her politically. That is not business— it is political manoeuvring.* (The idea of tainting business with politics must be as abhorrent to the business man as is the tainting of poetry with politics to the poet.)

Q. *Can you tell me something about this ' rationalizing' of Japanese industry which we hear so much of these days?*

A. *The whole trouble is insufficient exports. The pre-war population of Japan was sixty-eight million ; now it is nearing eighty-eight million. Yet our exports have reached only thirty-nine per cent of the pre-war level—whereas European countries have regained or exceeded their pre-war levels. Our export prices are too high, therefore we must reduce the cost of production by means of modernizing our machinery. This has already been accomplished to some extent. But then the trade unions promptly grabbed the profits—and so the export prices remained where they were.* (In the course of an article in the *Manchester Guardian* in May 1954, Hessell Tiltman said that the average monthly wage in all manufacturing industries in Japan was £17 7s., or about £12 if the Japanese yen were placed upon a more realistic exchange rate of 1,500 to the pound sterling. Mr. Tiltman summed up thus : ' Whatever the ultimate effects of post-war wage increases upon export prices, the average Japanese worker is still much where he was in the pre-war years—which was close to the subsistence level.') *But the basic weakness of the Japanese economy lies in the loss of her colonies and of China as a market.*

Q. *Is it still the practice of Japanese employers to keep on more workers than they really need, thus reducing unemployment?*

(This had always struck me as an admirable piece of 'paternalism'. Miss Tracy mentions that in 1949 when the *Asahi* newspaper was producing a daily two-page issue it had two thousand employees in Tokyo alone. Presumably the practice has the advantage of reducing the taxes paid to the government, and I get the impression that Japanese firms would rather do anything with their profits than dispose of them in that direction—would rather give them for instance to a geisha *okāsan* or the proprietor of an expensive cabaret; according to one report, the Tokyo District Tax Office estimated that it lost every year to tax-free company allowances some two hundred and thirty million pounds.)

A. *'Feather-bedding', as it's called—or 'concealed unemployment'? No, there is not very much of that going on these days.* (I was rather surprised by this answer, which was later confirmed by other Japanese to whom I spoke. Business is not good enough to allow of it, apparently. Nevertheless, by British standards the majority of Japanese companies are generously staffed. And a senior official of a large trading company told me that it was the custom with his firm to take a fresh batch of graduates every year from Waseda and other superior universities; for the first ten years or more these employees might be virtually useless, but they were 'carried' because later on some of their college coevals would hold important posts in the government service and in other spheres. This is not necessarily nepotism—the personal touch remains very important in Japanese business dealings, as elsewhere in Japanese life.)

Q. *Those of my students who are graduating this year are very nervous about finding posts in business. According to the press, sixty per cent or more of the country's new graduates are likely to be left jobless. Is this so?*

A. *Of course we are turning out far too many graduates— university men all looking for white-collar jobs. This is the fault of our post-war educational system. But they will all find some job, somewhere, there's no doubt about that.* (There are said to be nearly 600,000 unemployed in Japan, two-thirds of these living in Tokyo metropolis; but presumably there are still enough non-graduates in the country to account for this figure.)

Q. *What system of unemployment benefits have you in Japan?*

A. *Workers pay a certain percentage of their pay and employers also contribute; thus the unemployed draw a kind of dole. The arrangement varies from job to job, and many types of workers do not come into it at all. Certainly the system is less developed and regularized than in Britain.*

Q. *Perhaps this isn't fair—but do you think that industry can ever solve the problem of Japan's over-population?*

A. *We hear far too much about Japan's over-population. What does the word mean? In Tōjō's Japan people were encouraged to raise large families—that's what you call ' gun-fodder ', isn't it? And the same is happening in China at present. Japan is less densely populated than Britain—this talk is largely a myth—hot air.* (I never before bumped into so solid a myth, then—the trains crammed full, children scattered all over the roads, universities having to run duplicated evening courses to fit in their students. It is true that the Kansai is an exceptionally thickly populated area of the country. Even so the fact remains that in Japan, this buffer-state between east and west, the birth-rate is that of the orient while the death-rate is practically that of western Europe. In population density, Japan comes only third in the world, with 617 persons to the square mile. But in population density in ratio to cultivated land, Japan comes top, with 4,220 persons to the square mile. Where Britain cultivates eighty-five per cent of her land, Japan can cultivate only about fifteen per cent because of the extensive mountain ranges.) *One suggestion is that atomic energy might one day be used to level the mountain ranges and make the land arable. But what would most contribute to the solution would be expansion of foreign trade and the consequent expansion of industry. That, together with birth control, ought to solve what problem there is.* (One can understand his irritation: during the past twelve months more words have been devoted to the question of population control than to any other topic, excepting the H-bomb. Still, both topics are rather urgent. As regards the former, government nurses have made some progress in rural areas : the peasant's wife shows no objection at all, either social, moral or religious, to this aspect of applied science. This fact might seem encouraging. Until we discover that abortion is a traditional measure resorted to by the Japanese people in periods of emergency throughout their history. During the Tokugawa period, 1615–1853, the farmers' expression *mabiku*, to weed out, was much employed in the phrase *ko wo mabiku*, to weed out unwanted babies, and abortion houses, *chūjōryū*, hung out their signboards in the streets. According to an article written by Dr. Fumiko Y. Amano,[1] estimates of the number of abortions in the year 1950 range from 600,000 to a million, and for 1951 the figure of a million and a half to two million has been suggested, or nearly one abortion to every live birth. If contraceptive methods wipe out abortion it will be a great advance—but it may still leave the problem of population control untouched. Unfortunately the Japanese love children.)

Q. *What is the position of women in industry ?   Another amateurish question, I'm afraid . . .*

A. *The new Constitution established equal rights for women —but in practice women do not earn as much as men.   Equal pay for equal work would be a better way of describing the Constitution in its application to industry.*

Q. *Wasn't it a fact that women employees of the Ōmi Silk Spinning Company (estimated at ninety per cent of the total staff) were compelled to give up their work after marriage ?*

A. *The President, Mr. Natsukawa, held that the efficiency of married women was lower because of their other cares and interests.*

Q. *A case of 'Spinsters Only', then ?   But, talking about the Ōmi Silk dispute, the strangest thing to us foreigners is that*

[1] Vice-President of the Japan Birth League, in *Contemporary Japan*, Vol. XXI, Nos. 1–3, Tokyo, 1952.

Mr. Natsukawa compelled his workers to kneel once a week in front of the memorial tablets of his ancestors . . .

A. *There you go—just because it's Buddhism you foreigners make a fuss—if it were a question of kneeling in front of the Virgin Mary you wouldn't say a word—but Buddhism, that's heathen.*

Q. *You misunderstand me—I didn't know Buddhism came into it—at least, I thought it was Shinto—I only meant that it seemed strange to us that workers should have to pay their respects to their employer's dead family . . .* (The rebel union claimed that the company hymn which the employees had to sing every morning and the company oath which they had to recite every evening before going to bed both emphasized the Buddhist doctrine of self-denial and thus were intended to enervate the workers.)

A. *Hm. I agree that Mr. Natsukawa's behaviour in asking his workers to kneel before the memorial tablets was in very bad taste. I should certainly not wish to have my workers kneeling in front of my ancestral tablets!*

Q. *To move on to something more material—objection was brought against the dormitory facilities provided for the workers, wasn't it?*

A. *The girls themselves were quite satisfied—the trouble was caused by agitators, busybodies from outside. These girls come from very poor families and the dormitory life of the company was better than anything they had ever known.*

Q. *Were the dormitory facilities offered by this company of the same standard as those found in other firms of a similar size—and how did the wages compare?*

A. *The dormitory facilities were not quite up to the average level—and it is true that the wages were lower than those paid by comparable firms. But the Ōmi case is altogether exceptional in that, although it is a fairly large company, it has retained a number of the features of small companies—Mr. Natsukawa has been attempting to run a big business on the old paternalistic lines.* (Ōmi Silk Company was established by the present president's father in 1917, with 3,000 spindles; through Mr. Natsukawa's drive and acumen it is now a concern of 270,000 spindles and 12,000 employees.)

Q. *Mr. Natsukawa expressed himself as deeply shocked by the strike—do you believe in his good faith?*

A. *Yes, I think he is sincere—but mistaken.* (Mr. Natsukawa's behaviour is exactly that of one who has been outraged to the point of incredulity. His first recorded words on flying back to Japan from Paris are said to have been, ' This dispute is a revolt—it's a conspiracy ! The police are hand in glove with the union. Send the National Safety Force ! There are Communists among the news reporters ! I am going to fight this out till I smash the union, even if it means the ruin of the company ! ' In an interview which he accorded to Hessell Tiltman ' in order that the world may learn the truth ', Mr. Natsukawa stated, ' It is not an industrial dispute but a revolutionary uprising.' Mr. Tiltman ends his account, ' I left the air-conditioned comfort of the Ōmi Company's Tokyo office with the feeling that much the same arguments, justifications, and " explanations " were probably advanced by British employers a century ago.' [1] Mr. Natsukawa's ' paternalistic ' attitude is well illustrated by his quoted remark on overtime : ' It is silly to demand overtime—the same as a child asking its parents for pocket-money.' A rather Victorian father. I am reminded of the powerful industrialist, a kindly man and a good friend of mine, who, when asked whether his employees belonged to a union, replied, ' Oh yes, the one I established for them.' Overtime allowance was one of the rights demanded by the Ōmi strikers, together with holidays with pay, religious franchise, freedom to marry, termination of the practice of opening employees' mail and freedom to leave the premises after working hours— it was stated that seven chops or seals were required before a worker could leave the premises : the president did not want his children to fall into bad ways or into love. Certainly the Ōmi Silk Company is not a typical case—as Mr. Kōjirō Abe, president of the Tōyō Cotton Mills, has pointed out on behalf

[1] *Manchester Guardian Weekly,* 12 August 1954.

of other firms, with his voice aimed in the direction of Lanca-shire—but it is interesting in itself as a remnant of feudalism in an odd context. And what is even more interesting is that the state of affairs described by the union should have con-tinued to exist in a country which, according to the Rightists, is menaced by a Communist intelligentsia. One very good thing arising out of the dispute is that seventeen nations, led by British cotton workers, sent financial aid to the strikers. This is exactly what is wanted: for the sake of common humanity, and—since otherwise Japanese workers will be drawn increasingly to crude forms of Communism pivoting on Russia—for the sake of politics. It is not often that the two considerations coincide.)

Q. *I'm afraid you think that I introduced the Ōmi dispute as a kind of malicious red herring? But from what you say I see that the trouble lies in the fact that you are not exporting enough. It seems that you are not exporting enough because your prices are too high—and your prices are too high because you are not exporting enough. You have too many teachers teaching other people to become teachers ; you have too many poets turning out too much poetry for a non-existent market ; you have too many white-collar workers and not enough khaki-breeched workers —and yet you lack a market adequate to what your khaki-breeched workers can produce . . .* (In fact, that business is in a shocking state but business men as shrewd as my Business Man are doing reasonably well.)

A. *What you have just said is all very academic . . .*

THE ABBOT'S POINT OF VIEW

Everyone who is writing a book on Japan must be on the sharp lookout for an *éminence grise*. Miss Tracy spotted the Abbot of Nishi Honganji Temple in Kyoto and found him a devil. I was taken to see Zenkei Shibayama, the Abbot of Nanzenji Temple in Kyoto, and found him a man. An extremely lively man, and reassuringly sublunar. We drank tea and ate rice-cakes, and then the Abbot quite unaffectedly explained the more sensational aspects of Zen training : how he sat on his throne to expound the texts, how novices sometimes fell asleep during meditation and were then rapped smartly across the shoulders by the ' invigilator '—the Abbot laid vigorously about him with a sizeable stick and for a moment I felt alarm for our mutual friend, who was acting the culprit's part—and how, after such a chastisement, the novice and the master would bow shortly to each other and go about their business afresh.

From the *ʒendō*, with its two platforms of *tatami* on which the monks meditate and sleep, we returned to the Abbot's private room, sparsely furnished with a low table and fans and cushions for the visitors. A novice brought in cups of sweet cocoa. It was a fine summer's day. Outside, the crickets were grinding industriously away and a novice's shears were clicking as he cut a hedge—but it seemed a new world, of utter and sudden silence, after the tapping of cobblers' hammers in the *eta* district through which we had just come, and the cajoling old women outside the brothels along the Kamogawa, and the racket and rattle of the traffic-jammed streets of the ancient capital. Behind us in the garden was a luxuriantly flowering tree : *ryōshōka*, which the dictionary translates into ' great trumpet flower ' : framed in the open *shōji*, its branches were hung with unbelievable colours. The Abbot's face was pleasantly mobile, his eyes sparkled, he really seemed to be all there. One did not get the impression that he was half of him inextricably lost in some fathomless *haiku* or that, under cover of the cocoa, he was thinking up a smart piece of Zen repartee. Had the Abbot any ideas about this world and this time ? He definitely had.

There were three paths for Japan to follow at present, the Abbot said, seriously but without pomposity. Alliance with Russia, or alliance with America, or the third way which those who chose to misunderstand it call ' neutralism '. He seemed unconvinced that either of the first two ways could be said to be ' preferable ' to the other. Nehru, he considered, should be Japan's example. He went on to point out that the choice of such a policy would not be easy to sustain : Japan would have to forgo the perquisites of co-operation with a wealthy power. Moreover, she would be obliged to build up an adequate social security scheme—something after the British model—if her independent stand were to have any real meaning. If this could be done, then Japan would be able to take her place, along with India and Britain, as an influential ' Third Force '. (The feeling of the ordinary Japanese towards the idea of a future war is very similar to that of the ordinary British. Britain is recovering from a successful war, and Japan—less certainly—from an unsuccessful one. The people of both nations suspect that another war, whether they were on the winning or on the losing side, would be fatal to their existence. The British feel that in a nuclear war they would be the first casualty ; and the Japanese feel that they themselves are already the first nuclear casualty. The difference is that in Japan the extremists on both wings are more vocal than they would be in a country enjoying a reasonable degree of social stability—that state which Lafcadio Hearn said the Japanese had no need of—and they receive more attention. When you have little to live for, it is not very hard to die. I think the Abbot would agree with what Professor W. Macmahon Ball writes in a recent issue of the *English Mainichi* : ' For my part, I greatly hope that Japan will not work out her foreign policy in terms of her potential military power, but rather in terms of her actual and potential economic power. Because of Japan's social and political structure I doubt whether she can become militarized without becoming militaristic . . . It seems to me that it is by their economic skills, not their military prowess, that the Japanese people can best assure security and welfare both for themselves and for their neighbours in the Pacific.')

The Abbot admitted that on the surface his policy held out few attractions. He could not offer either guns or butter— they are apt to come in the same parcel these days. Yet I think that his policy does recommend itself to the widespread desire of the Japanese for independence of both America and

Russia and to the chastened patriotism of the middle classes.
The Abbot's immediate influence, as a religious leader, is small
—confined, that is, to his parishioners.   But through articles
written for the national Japanese dailies, he reaches a very
considerable audience, and he is well-known for speaking out.

After the ' realism ' of the business men's statesmen and the
' idealism ' of the intellectuals, it was refreshing to find, in a
Buddhist priest, a measured attitude which was humane without being hysterical and sober without being cynical.   The
only embarrassing part of our interview lay in the difficulty I
found in explaining to the Abbot, at his request, wherein lay
the differences between Anglicanism, Catholicism and the
other chief sects of Christianity, and why these differences
could not be shelved in the face of a common crisis.

HAPPY NEW YEAR

An avalanche of cards, a thousand calligraphic miles,
    assure a bright New Year.
And yet and yet, I met a banker weeping through his smiles,
    upon that hectic morn.

Omedetō, he told me, while the saké bubbled on his lips.
His frock-coat trembled in its new and yearly bliss.
' A hard year for Japan,' he said, and gurgled out a sigh.
' A hard grim year.' A saké-smelling tear suffused his
    reddened eye.

He clapped me by the hand, he led me to his bright new
    house.
He showed his ancient incense burners, precious treasures,
    cold and void.
His family too he showed, drawn up in columns, and his
    fluttering spouse.
We bowed and wept together over the grim new year.

I walked away, my head was full of yen, of falling yen.
I saw the others with their empty pockets,
Merry on the old year's dregs, their mouths distilled a warm
    amen !

The poor are always with us. Only they
    can find a value in the new.
They are the masters of their fourpenny kites
That soar in the open market of the sky.
Whatever wrongs await, they still preserve some rites.

14 : A HUMAN SCRAPBOOK

> 'The world of dew
> Is a world of dew and yet,
> And yet.'
> *(Issa, trans. Donald Keene)*

THE poet had lost his only child. This world is a floating cloud, it passes like the drops of dew, he agreed with the friends who were trying to comfort him—and yet . . .

And yet happiness is real, and so is sorrow. To record the happiness and the sorrows of the ordinary Japanese family is clearly beyond my poor abilities. But in this chapter I had hoped to gather material, not only illustrating the subjects raised in other chapters, but also relating to the more striking and therefore more amenable comedies and tragedies of everyday life in contemporary Japan. But looking now at my scrapbook, I see that the tragedies far outweigh the comedies. Whether this preponderance is fairly due to my theme of Japan or whether it is an unfair consequence of that gloom which seems to be an occupational disease of writers whatever their nationality, I am in no position to inform the reader.

The dates of the press cuttings are indicated so that readers will see that they pertain to a short period of time and are not exotic items pursued curiously through years of newspaper files. I have supplied no more than a necessary minimum of comment.

(October 1954)

'A fortune tellers' society, first of its kind in Japan, was organized in Kyoto. There are seventy members in the club. Present at the opening ceremony was Governor Ninagawa of Kyoto Prefecture.

'Purpose : To publish pamphlets and calendars and hold lectures and classes to uplift the personality of the mind readers and elevate their position socially and economically.'

(A letter to Asahi Shimbun, September 1954)

'My fellow-workers and I are nurses at a national hospital. I am convinced the work of looking after those who are sick is noble. But once we take off our nurse's white uniform and change into ordinary attire, we are no different from other girls. Yet hospital regulations say nurses are not allowed to fall in love and should by no means fall in love with a patient. Even walking with a member of the other sex is frowned upon as smearing the prestige of the hospital. . . .

'Is our demand for freedom in love based on a misunderstanding of what freedom means ? If the ban is based on the fact that we assist in treating precious human life, then why is it that doctors are free to fall in love and marry ? '

(From a composition by Shunichi Eguchi, 15)

'The other day when we had a discussion at school about whether our Emperor is a war criminal or not, I began to think again about my father . . .

'One day a little package was delivered to us. It contained a tiny wine cup from the Emperor, a present to us because our father had been killed in the war. My little brother, only seven, began to cry. "Who wants an old wine cup ? " he sobbed angrily. "They killed our father. We want our father." Mother looked anxious and tried to quiet him, but we all had the same feeling in our hearts. . . . When we grow up we must do something to keep our country from ever going to war again.' [1]

(From a composition by Kōichi Eguchi, 14)

'. . . Our poverty is not due to inability or laziness. It is

[1] From *Echoes from a Mountain School*, compositions collected by Seikyō Muchaku, teacher of Yamamoto village school, Yamagata Prefecture, and translated by G. Caulfield and M. Kimura (Kenkyusha Ltd., Tokyo, 1953).

simply because we haven't enough land. How can a family of five subsist on two-thirds of an acre of land? There is nothing ahead but a losing struggle and final destitution. It was the fate of my father and mother and will probably be mine. . . .

'Tomorrow is the thirty-fifth day after mother's death. I will report all these things to her spirit. I will also promise her that I will study hard and try to find out why she had to work so hard with so little result and why people cannot earn enough to live on, even if they work every minute as she did. I also want to find out if I can buy a rice field without causing the man who sells it to suffer . . .'[1]

(August 1953)

' The Japan Red Cross Friday evinced it would secede from the Executive Committee for the Consolation of Souls of Dead Chinese POWs, denouncing the latter for being too Leftist-inclined.'

(June 1954)

' " Dai Nippon Seisan-tō " (which literally means the Great Japan Production Party), one of the most powerful Rightist groups, was formally revived Monday, June 28th, when its first post-war convention was held at Nakanoshima Central Public Hall in Osaka.

' This is said to be one of the steps for the Japanese Rightists to cement their yet fluid and often disunited fronts into one compact and co-ordinated force. Toshiharu Kawakami was elected at the convention as the first post-war leader and the third since its inception 23 years ago. Kawakami is the head of the Anti-Communization Group which was formed in May 1952. He was also one of the leaders of the former Black Dragon Association (Kokuryū-kai). . . . As of June 24th, the party covers forty prefectures with over 6,000 regular members.

' Kawakami in his address to 500 participants from all parts of Japan clarified five reasons to " re-establish " the party.

[1] From *Echoes from a Mountain School.*

They were : (1) To break the deadlock which Japan is now facing under incomplete independence and semi-colonial status ; (2) To establish a political and economic stability based on moral justice ; and to stamp out the evils deeply rooted in Japan's political parties, government officials, Zaibatsu and the intelligentsia ; (3) To cope with the Communist bloc which is trying to divide the world into two parts and finally to occupy Japan ; (4) To reform capitalism drastically ; (5) To go hand in hand with other Asian countries.'

(September 1954)

' Ultra-nationalist leaders who terrorized the country with successive acts of terrorism in the early 1930's strutted out of the post-war obscurity and harangued in packed Kyōritsu Auditorium in Tokyo Monday.

' Occasionally swinging fists, they ominously warned the audience that " only by resorting to political terrorism could we get rid of political corruption and chaos ".

' One of the speakers, Kashō Sagaya, who shot Prime Minister Yūkō Hamaguchi to death at Tokyo Central Station in December 1930, groaned that " we have only three alternatives to cope with the Liberal administration which is playing havoc with the nation's legislature by virtue of its numerical superiority. First, to arouse public opinion against the Yoshida Administration," he spelled out, " secondly, to invoke the Emperor's absolute authority to force an en masse resignation of the existing Cabinet, and in the third place, to resort to political terrorism ".

' Brushing aside the first two measures as " impracticable at the present time ", ethnocentrist Sagaya deplored that recourse to terrorism is the " only alternative left for us to wipe out the current political corruption ". He recalled that in 1930 when he assassinated the stubborn Prime Minister, one business firm after another was collapsing under the austerity economic policy, and cases of suicides and insanity were swelling up.

'Other speakers included Nisshō Inoue who from behind the scenes wire-pulled a series of Rightist uprisings and acts of terrorism, Tadashi Konuma who assassinated the late Finance Minister Junnosuke Inoue in April 1932, and former Navy Ensign Haruo Ōba who participated in the May 15th Incident in 1932.

'The " Let's-Unveil-the-Truth " meeting was sponsored by the Gokoku-dan (National Protection League)—one of the post-war Rightist organizations, with an estimated membership of 30,000, the keynote of whose political platform has been the " negation of individualism ".'

(A Japanese commentator, August 1954)

'Questioned as to who the Emperor was, most school children confessed to their ignorance of him. While " I don't know " was the typical reply, a girl in the sixth grade said : " He was formerly a god but is now a simple commoner. He is much happier as he now is." Nowadays, school children do not learn anything about the Emperor at all until they reach the sixth grade. This is, indeed, a vast change compared with the pre-war education.

'The Emperor may be happy and content " as he now is " but the question is : What will be the attitude of these children to the Tennō system when they grow into mature citizens ? On the answer to this question may depend the ultimate relations between the Imperial House and the people at large. All that can be said at this moment is that the Tennō system has well survived the shock of defeat and the Emperor holds his position securely as a constitutional monarch, though he dons an entirely new garb.'

(September 1954)

'The Government at the Cabinet meeting Wednesday decided to establish a Japanese version of the Un-American Activities Commission—the Anti-Democratic Movements Prevention Council. The newly established organ of the Government will operate under the presidency of Deputy

Prime Minister Taketora Ogata. The council, it was announced, is purported to work out prompt and efficient counter-measures against all sorts of activities detrimental to the sound development of democracy in this country.

'The council consists of Ministers of Justice, Foreign Affairs, Education, Agriculture and Forestry, Labour, Police Superintendent, Director-General of Defence Agency and the Chief Cabinet Secretary. Members of the council will meet regularly to ensure proper co-ordination of joint operations among themselves.'

(A letter to Hokkaidō Shimbun, Sapporo, August 1954)

'I thought it a shame that the small Japanese paper flags used to welcome the Emperor were thrown away so I began to pick them up on my way home. I was astounded to find someone using one as a handkerchief to blow his nose. To think that only a few minutes ago they had been waved in frenzied welcome. I felt sad over the people's indifference regarding the national emblem . . .'

(October 1954)

'The Osaka Prefectural Education Board Friday demanded of the Osaka chapter of the Japan Teachers Union to withdraw its instruction calling for a silent-prayer of school pupils for the late Aikichi Kuboyama, history's first H-bomb victim, on the occasion of his funeral services on October 9th.

'The instruction issued on October 2nd as part of the union's anti-hydrogen bomb campaign also urged principals and teachers to make speeches in memory of the late Kuboyama on the day.

'The education board interpreted the union's move as intervention in education and as an attempt to place education under the union's control. In the meantime, the Hyōgo chapter of the Japan Teachers Union Friday also instructed all the schools in Hyōgo Prefecture to urge pupils, their guardians and teachers to write letters of condolence to Mrs. Kuboyama and Miss Sayo Kuboyama, youngest daughter.'

(March 1954)

' The Tachikawa chapter of the extreme Left-wing Japan Teachers Union called on the mayor of Tachikawa to prohibit the attendance of local Japanese school children at the annual Christmas party given by the U.S. Far East Air Material Command . . .   The reason given for the union's stand was reported to be that the participation in the Christmas programme was a violation of the Fundamental Education Law, which prohibits religious activities in the schools . . .'

(A letter to Asahi Shimbun, from a student of Osaka University, February 1954)

' There is a university which has come out stating that it was boycotting Marxist economics.   This was revealed by a professor speaking over a commercial broadcasting station on the " School Hour ".   He said that some among the students were indulging in academic controversies, being the victims of the agitation of a minority.   And after four years of sponging on their parents for tuition, they are unable to get employment.   The professor pointed out that the outstanding feature of his institution was that it boycotted Marxist economics.   He added that an automobile course was an extra feature of the school, besides other practical studies which would enable the students to work in banks and stores from the very next day after leaving school.   I was flabbergasted at this one-sided attitude . . .'

(The following poem, by Riichi Noda, a poet in his mid-forties, comes from a recent issue of the ' modernist' anthology, ' Wasteland'.   In translation its distinctively Japanese turn of phrase and whatever it possesses by way of aural beauty have been lost ; and moreover the translator's modest ambition to give a ' literal' English version was frustrated at several points by the obscurity of the original.   Nevertheless I think it conveys some impression of the kind of tone and the species of imagery common to much contemporary ' foreign-style' Japanese poetry.   In form, the verse is ' free'.   Readers should allow for the fact that, in trans-

*lation, the element of ' adoption' is stressed at the expense of that
of ' adaptation'.)*

CHORUS OUT OF CRISIS

I

Lost in dust,
                    What is lost?
—It will be meaning in the mind—
Safe we are in the corrupt air of the tube until we reach our
        destination.
                    Who is safe?
—It will be the runaway's psychology—
In the human mind another Sphinx buries part of itself beneath the
        sand and the antenna grasps the call-sign jammed in peace as
        if between wars of death.
We noises.   We sparks.
It is the dance of petroleum that we dance.   Dance of pay increases.
Dance of rayon staple.   Dance of errors.
—Not the footsteps of the universe, not the sobbings ; the sounds
        will be nothing but a single return-ticket—
We dance as three persons, dance as ten persons.
Our dance is the dancing of skins.   Dancing of counter-light.
        Dancing of wave-motion.
                    One person knows the remaining nine persons.
We are one.   We are one.
Do you know that tidal wave, friend on the right side ?   Yesterday
        I was ' custom ' on board the yacht and you the fish caught
        up on the rod.
Do you know that shudder, friend on the left side ?   Today you
        are a house-maid and I a plate to be dropped and broken out
        of your hand.
Who, tomorrow, will be a skilled physician and we the hopeless
        cases ?

2

Our claws meet with each other's hurried exit
What will the eye-witness see ?
Refugees, where will they find their refuge ?
    o

Though we keep our diary and synchronize our watches, of a
    sudden sorrow comes
                    Though we support our sorrow in our hands
It will not be the stove that warms our hearts without warning
Substance evades us, there is a dark vacant lot in our purpose
Above all morning groans and evening goes mad
We hold up all the reptiles' feet, trace back irregularly butterflies'
    mutations every day, and have recourse to insects' antennae
    on the spot
We retardation   we leakage
Fission will be our tickets
                    Union will be divided until re-united
Ah busy   entirely busy   there are benches to be sat on   there are
    newspapers to be read in
But confusions of confusions   Where am I now in the world?
We demagogues   we sum total
It is a chronic fight that we fight   fight of the seamy side
Fight of deferment   fight of recollections
It is the fight of ants that we fight eternally
(Or shall I say 'like an intermittent siesta dream among sand-
    bags'?
Or shall I say 'like a phantom transient and gyrating of "the
    forest of earth and concrete"
                    from out of the desolation
                    from out of the desolation'?) [1]

(August 1954)
    'In Kyoto a lady professor won a doctorate in medicine
with a very womanly thesis on "How to Cook Potato".
Five years ago a bespectacled nutrition expert, H—— B——,
of Dōshisha Women's College, decided it was high time
for women to attack the potato scientifically.   The distin-

----

[1] 'Counter-light': a term from photography (one of the
popular arts of contemporary Japan)—'taken into the light',
therefore blurred.
    '"custom"': 'conventional usage', used in a pejorative
sense.
    'our claws': as of robots.
    '"the forest of earth and concrete"'—'the asphalt jungle'?

guished School of Medicine, Kyoto University, served out the
doctorate.'

(*The following is an ' existentialist sketch ' which a research
student honoured my wife with, after she had given a series of
lectures on contemporary French literature at one of the ex-
Imperial universities. He excused his ' grammatical errors '
on the grounds that he had ' neglected ' the Carthusian father who
gave exercises in French conversation because he (the father, that
is) was a Christian, adding ' Je voudrais préférer l'humaniste,
simplement, naïf, ou bien l'existantialiste [sic], ou bien l'humaniste
classique.'*)

' Dieu (qui est mon ami)
  Un jeune homme (comme moi)

Un jeune homme.—Mon Dieu ! J'ai me tué !

Dieu.—Quoi ?

Un j.h. (hausse les épaules)—J'ai abandonné ma vie, mon
 être : j'ai cessé d'aimer, aimer la vie.
     (*Silence*)

Dieu.—C'est ta faute, c'est tout.

Un j.h.—Faute ?

Dieu.—Oui, tu ne peut être que tu étais, et tu es. Cesser
 d'être c'est de négliger ta vie.

Un j.h.—Oui, j'ai negligé ma vie, mais pourtant, j'ai me tué,
 ma vie ; c'est moi que m'a tué.

Dieu.—Ça. Ça. Bien. Tu t'a reserré si étroitement dans
 tes circonstances. Tu n'en fuis pas. Tu étais drôle.

Un j.h.—Si ! J'étais drôle, méchant . . . c'est moi.

Dieu.—Ton corps injuré ne peut guérir, jamais.

Un j.h.—J'en connais bien . . .

Dieu.—Toi ! Tu n'es pas mort, tu vis . . .

Un j.h.—Oui (hausse les épaules) Je devais vivre avec ce
 corps injuré, injuré par moi.

Dieu.—C'est toi qui es obligeant à cette faute.

Un j.h.—Oui, mais cependant quoi je pouvais ? J'avais ma
 vie heureuse et libre peut-être. J'ai perdu mon espoir

à future, et néanmoins je dois vivre, dans la même circonstance comme autrui, journalière peut-être. J'ai tombé dans la plus mauvaise. (Silence) J'étais folle. (Dieu se perd.)
la fin.'

(*A letter from a girl who had been taking French lessons from my wife*)

' Now, I have to write that I cannot but give up learning French because our family is in the trouble.   As I mentioned in previous letter, my sister has been sick and her X-ray examination found that her sick is a kind of Caries.   She is going to be sent to hospital before long.

' I have never thought that I should quit the lesson so soon, and I might be unable to finish even a general course.   Since my family had repatriated from China on 1946, we have been in eventful life.   Therefore, I am used to throw away my own hope or desire by home trouble.   I am afraid, however, that you might be disappointed and you do not like such manner. I hope you will understand me though my explanation is very poor.

' Allow me to repeat that I am sorry, and in spite of your deep kindness to me, I have to give up the lesson, which will be valuable memory.   Although I know it is very impudent to you, I wish I might regain your lesson upon the recovering of my sister.

' Thank you very much for the kind leading.   I will never forget your family and the happiness I could be acquainted with you.

' Wishing everlasting peace and happiness upon your family,

I am
Yours very faithfully . . .'

(An Atom-bomb poem ; by Tōge Sankichi, 1917–1953)

AT THE EMERGENCY DRESSING STATION

' You
Who though you weep have no outlet for the tears
Who though you groan have no lips for words
Who though you writhe have no skin on your clutching fingers
You

You wave your limbs stained in blood and greasy sweat and lymph,
Whitely flash your eyes drawn thin as strings
Hold around your swollen bellies nothing more than the elastic of
    your drawers
You who can no longer even hide your parts of shame—
Ah, who could believe it true
That you were all until a moment ago
Lovable girl-students ?
From within the darkly fluttering flames
Of Hiroshima burnt and infected,
You who are no longer yourselves
One after another jumping out, crawling out,
Made your way to this grassy field,
And bury your roasted heads of bacon in the dust of agony.

Why did you have to meet such a fate ?
Why did you have to meet such a fate ?
For what purpose ?
For what purpose ?
You still are not aware
How far your appearance is already
Removed from humankind.

Only thinking,
You are thinking,
Of your father, mother, brother, sister,
You saw just this morning
(If they met you now who would recognize you ?)
Of your house where you got up from sleep and ate

(In an instant the flowers on the fence were wrenched off, and
　　now you could not tell even the ashes)
You are thinking
Lying between creatures like you who one after another stop
　　moving,
That once you were a girl,
Once you were a human girl.'

*(The following is an extract from a comment by the present
writer on a newspaper article by a Japanese poetess, Sumako
Fukao, printed in the ' English Mainichi' in November 1954)*

'It was interesting to read Miss Fukao's article, *Poets and
Death Ash*, urging Japanese poets to raise their voices against
nuclear weapons, but I must confess that the usefulness of her
advice seems very doubtful to me.

'As Miss Fukao implies, there has been a certain dilettantism
about Japanese poets in the past : they contrived to withdraw
only too completely from the world of ordinary mortals.
This withdrawal did not ' purify' or ' spiritualize' their
poetry in any valuable way : it merely conventionalized both
what they said and how they said it . . .　The predominant
imagery of *tanka* and *haiku* was of course ' natural '—' natural '
as distinct from ' human ', for the latter tended to be excluded
as trivial, unworthy and even a little on the squalid side.
Blossom, the moon, fireflies, cicadas, pines, frogs and ancient
ponds—this imagery was put to its fullest use, but the poetry
characterized by it remained at a safe distance from normal
human interests.

'The situation has now changed.　Japanese poets, as Miss
Fukao puts it, " have leaped into the world arena ".　They
have turned their attention from the noise of the cicadas to
the noise of exploding bombs.　But what about the life between ?　What about that great and important stretch of
common experience which lies between the two extremes of
cicada and bomb ?　Is this to be passed over in silence ?　If
so, I cannot believe that the " poetic revolution " in Japan
will be a genuine one.

'Observation of departments of life quite other than literature may suggest that the Japanese, when they depart from some traditional way of thinking or behaving, are inclined to swing violently to the opposite extreme. So that, in many cases, the last state bears a curious resemblance to the first: the form has changed drastically, but the spirit remains much the same. If this should happen in poetry, then the H-bomb will merely turn out to be the modern poet's substitute for the cicada, and the mushroom cloud of its explosion only his latter-day equivalent of the cone of Mount Fuji. That is, the "nuclear weapon" may transpire to be nothing more than a conventional image, a *cliché*, which its users falsely suppose to be inherently poetic—on the lines of "Any H-bomb poem is a good poem". . . .

'The amount of literature devoted to the H-bomb is already so immense that I can see no reason why poets should be obliged to add their unimportant quota. It seems to me that they would be better occupied in pursuing their own humanity and in trying to say something significant both of and for secular humanity. Otherwise Japanese poets will only succeed in making the H-bomb appear more important than the human beings who may drop it or on whom it may be dropped. Something of this nature is already happening . . .'

(September 1954)

'One evening last week a man offering to sell his own life, silently shuffled along in Hibiya Park, Tokyo. The man, middle-aged and having the appearance of a shabby construction worker, refused to divulge the secret behind his strange deal that offers his life for ¥50,000 (£50).

'The garishly painted price tag bobbed along incongruously as the macabre merchant wended his way among the pleasure-seeking young lovers that crowded the park late until dusk.'

(September 1954)

'At about 1.30 a.m. a thirteen or fourteen-year-old boy

was found suffering in front of Nakanoshima Public Hall by a policeman. The youth was treated at a hospital but died at 2 p.m. the same day. He had taken rat poison.

' Just before his death he faintly related the tragic story of his short life. He gave his name as Kazuo Yamamoto, age thirteen. He became an orphan through war ravage and was sent to an orphanage in Tokyo. Leaving the orphanage, he had been earning his living shining shoes before coming to Osaka on September 1st.

' His last words were : " I wanted to die because of a headache." He had no personal belongings with him.'

(August 1954)

' Kazuhiro Tanaka, 29, guard of the Katsura Detached Palace, Kyoto, committed suicide with his pistol in a bamboo bush of the palace yesterday at 7.30 p.m.

' He was an enthusiastic Christian. The main cause of his suicide is believed to be his failure to maintain a religious way of living.'

(January 1954)

' Tokyo police yesterday reported the third case in three days of a double suicide pact in which one partner died and the other remained in a critical condition.

' In the latest suicide pact were J—— S——, twenty-one-year-old Waseda student, and his nineteen-year-old class-mate, K—— T——. The youth was found dead in the gas-filled apartment room of Miss T——, who was unconscious. Both left suicide notes indicating that general mental depression prompted them to end their lives.'

(October 1954)

' The daughter of a police lieutenant and her lover, a construction worker, both of them twenty-five years old, ended their lives with dynamite in a hotel room in front of the Tateyama (Chiba) railway station today.

' Their shattered remains were found together with a blood-

stained will which read : " Please combine our wedding and
funeral in one ceremony. Please bury us together."
  ' Both had been suffering from tuberculosis.'

(*February 1954*)

  ' After the last showing of the Japanese war film " Goodbye
Rabaul " at the Nichigeki Theatre in downtown Tokyo last
night, an attendant saw a young man apparently asleep in the
last row. He shook him and said the show was over.
  ' He was startled when he felt the hands were icy cold and
found there was no pulse. An empty box of sleeping pills
and emptied bottle of orangeade were found at his feet. A
note saying only " Death is sweet " was also found.'

(*August 1954*)

  ' In Nishinomiya a man committed suicide simply because
he had become " sick " of the present government.
  ' Police identified the pessimist whose poisoned body was
found in an abandoned building as a shipper's winch driver,
aged forty. To eliminate any mystery as to the cause of his
death, the suicide had cautiously left behind a note that read :
" I have become so sick and tired of this world and the Yoshida
government . . ." '

(*July 1954*)[1]

  ' Mrs. S—— T—— (51) hanged herself in her home in
Minami Ward, Osaka, last Saturday. Her husband and other

  [1] 'Pachinko' (pin-ball) has been described as 'Japan's semi-
original existentialist contribution to the world of " entertainment"'. Fresh pachinko parlours go up every day ; some streets
consist almost entirely of them, on both sides. They are always
well patronized ; the incessant ringing of the balls is certainly like
some minor kind of existentialist hell. It is said that in one such
establishment a patron suffered a heart attack and fell down dead,
but no one noticed until long afterwards, as they were all absorbed
in the game. One parlour in Kobe City is embellished with caged

members of the family told the police Mrs. T—— was obsessed
with the pachinko game for the past two years and had spent
her money as well as incurring debts to play the pin-balls. The
police accepted the cause of death as a suicide induced
by temporary insanity resulting from excessive pachinko
addiction.'

(*May 1954*)

' Tokyo Metropolitan Police disclosed yesterday, following
the confession by a sex maniac of the rape-slaying of a seven-
year-old girl, that 13,650 sex perverts, most of whom are dope
addicts, are on their blacklist. How many more thousands
there are throughout the country is a matter of conjecture.'

singing birds inside and a small black bear, also caged, outside.
The balls are twenty-five for a shilling, and the prizes take the form
of cigarettes, razor blades, soap and foodstuffs, which are often
sold back, through a ' broker ', to the manager of the parlour.

According to an Osaka police report, there are 1,001 pachinko
establishments in the city, patronized by 370,000 Osakans daily
(out of a total population of 2,400,000), and each patron spends an
average of ¥130 (1s. 7d.) per day—a daily total of ¥48,511,370
(£48,500 odd). Roughly thirty per cent of the Osaka halls are
operated by Chinese or other foreigners. The Osaka police report
225 cases of juvenile crime due to pachinko influence in the six
months covered ; 85 fights between patrons ; two suicides and one
attempted suicide ; nine divorces and two cases of wives running
away from their husbands.

A Japanese delegate to the Conference of the Institute of Pacific
Relations held in Kyoto in 1954 explained the phenomenon as a
result of the abolition of the family system. In that case one can
hope that these hordes of lost children will soon find other sub-
stitutes ; judging from the joyless expression on the faces of the
players, pachinko is an unpleasant drug to swallow, though
obviously effective, up to a point. The rich man has his cabaret
and his geisha ; the middling income man has his beer and his bar-
girl ; and the poor man has his pachinko. It would hardly be fair
to inveigh against the latter alone ; it is not a cause but an effect,
of that general instability which we have noticed elsewhere.

(October 1954)

' A seventeen-year-old high school girl, daughter of a comparatively well-off family, in January began forming a group
of girls to work in cabarets (" arbeit salons ") where they were
employed as " amateur " hostesses . . . The young girls
were so thrilled by the night life they had entered and so keen
on making customers they began to go out with some of their
customers over-night.

' Many of the young girls, working in establishments in
Ginza and Kanda, became wild and took to using drugs and
staying at questionable hotels in their efforts to hold on to
their patrons. Police first caught on to these wild, promis-
cuous teen-agers when several of them became pregnant and
some were arrested for stealing lingerie and clothes with
which to make themselves more attractive to their customers.'

(September 1954)

' About half of the 250 citizens who attended the ceremony
to console the spirits of the war dead here (Ōmi-Hachiman)
yesterday were stricken with food poisoning late last night.
Their condition was declared not serious. The cause is said
to be from eating lunch prepared by a *sushi* (rice and raw fish
" sandwich ") shop.'

(September 1954)

' To put the chill on overly heated customers, amorous or
otherwise, the geisha girls of Kyoto have an answer. Swelter-
ing customers are treated to a magically small fan which can
be stored in the entertainers' handbags.

' This contribution to the Atomic age à la Japanese style
consists of two small feathers that quickly whirl around by
pushing a button. Priced at a mere ¥300 (6s.), the pint-sized
breeze builder has created a storm among the clientele.'

(September 1954)

' *Pen Pals Wanted:* Y—— M——, Kudamatsu City,
Yamaguchi Prefecture. Age 27. Interested in Jesus Christ,

music, table tennis. Would like to correspond with any person in any country.'

(September 1954)

'In view of the rapid soaring of the prices of canned goods, candles, nails, wooden boards, and other commodities due to the approaching typhoon, the Hyōgo prefectural and municipal police authorities have issued orders to control profiteering.'

(September 1954)

'Weathermen in Tokyo complained last week that they have been completely exhausted by the rapid series of typhoons. For their painstaking sleepless days and nights, the overtime budget for the scores of employees totalled a meagre £100. In some local observatories, the amount is as low as 10s. for twenty hard-working scientists.

'"For every typhoon, we lose at least eight pounds in weight," a hollow-cheeked weatherman complained.'

(October 1954)

'In a statement he had penned, Mr. Yasujirō Tsutsumi, Japan's Lower House Speaker and celebrated jiujitsu expert, gave a belated explanation about the well-publicized parliamentary "mystery": Why did he fail to use judo and toss rioters from windows in the last Diet free-for-all?

'"I could, if I wanted to, use judo as much as I liked," Mr. Tsutsumi wrote, "they were all so defenceless."

'In the appalling mêlée which, occurring on the night of June 3rd, had forced the postponement of Premier Yoshida's trip abroad, the Speaker fainted and had to be carried out for medical treatment. In disgust some newspapers both at home and abroad hinted he was no blackbelter (sixth grade) but a fake.

'"For anyone well-versed in the art of judo," Mr. Tsutsumi continued, "it would have been the easiest thing to administer *atemi* (a deadly judo punch). But it would necessarily have caused murder and for me as a Speaker to indulge in such violence was out of the question."

' Explaining why he had to be carried off the Diet floor, Mr. Tsutsumi added : " My friends were afraid that in the confusion I might lose my head and be forced to use the deadly art. That is why they forced me out of the scene."

' As an afterthought, however, Mr. Tsutsumi said judo for him was very " handy " in that it inculcated patience in him : " To listen to all these long-winded speeches at the Speaker's seat requires so much patience ".'

(June 1954)

' The Audrey Hepburn hair-style craze, spreading like wildfire from one end of Japan to the other, yesterday caused beauty parlour operators in Kokura City, Kyūshū, to pause in the midst of the unexpected windfall, to sponsor a religious ceremony to ask forgiveness for having " tortured " so many locks.

' It is a custom to hold " kuyō " or Buddhist memorial services for the repose of the souls of all animate and inanimate things which have had to be sacrificed for the happiness of mankind . . .'

15 : AND YET, AND YET . . .

> ' Far better, it seems, than uttering pompous words
> And looking wise,
> To drink saké and weep drunken tears'
> *(Ōtomo Tabito, eighth century)*

So what should Japan do ? Like Francis Haar's documentary on student life, this book has no solution to offer. The condition of the country is such that the imagination boggles, it tries to pull itself together, it starts to suggest that some fifty per cent of the population should undergo compulsory euthanasia. . . .

But the Japanese are fond of proverbs, and we have one that says, 'Take care of the pennies . . .' There are many little abuses which Japan could put right. She might start, where there is no obstacle, with the small things. Spitting in public places could be prohibited and severely punished, since it is both unaesthetic and unhygienic, and the latter property at any rate is absolute and universal. Public urination might be made an offence for the same reasons, and more so. Thirdly, people who throw out unwanted animals should be fined heavily. This is not a manifestation of English sentimentality on the point of dumb animals, but a suspicion that cruelty is one and indivisible and that lack of feeling for our four-footed friends is likely to be accompanied by a lack of feeling for our two-footed ones. Fourthly, if I may change my tack, little boys should be treated with less sentimentality and slapped as often as seems advisable ; for it appears unlikely that a responsible and decent manhood will grow out of an inconsiderate, loutish and utterly uncontrolled boyhood.

No one has asked me for advice, but I intend to give a piece all the same. It would be a great advance if the Japanese could cease to worry so much over their ' traditions ', if they could rid themselves of that persistently self-conscious attitude towards their own past. I am forever being told that some Japanese tradition or other is in danger. Apparently the Americans, with their enthusiasm for applied democracy, are mainly responsible for this—though today the Americans are busily flattering the prettier of those same traditions and thereby administering to the fallacy that Japan is a unique nation composed of something other than normal human beings. What a ridiculous situation it is ! Are the Japanese such a feeble race that they will collapse at the loss of a few ambiguous traditions ? I suspect that, among other things, it is their peculiar reluctance to cut their losses which is at present impeding their efforts to carry out social reforms. Even the most liberal thinkers appear to have one foot stuck fast to the ground, willing to reform and yet afraid to change the pattern. To talk of ' dying traditions ' is a masterpiece of cruel mockery at a time when the newspapers carry almost every day a fresh story of a whole family wiping itself out because the struggle to survive has become unbearable.

The Japanese have had Shintō, the Way of the Gods ; and Bushidō, the Way of the Warrior ; and Kōdō, the Way of the Emperor. What they might try now is the Way of the Human. All the circumstances are against them. Yes. But circumstances will not change until there has been a change of heart. If the Japanese can finally liberate themselves from the past and survive the present, they should do great things. There is an unused fund of virtue in them.

A MOMENT OF HAPPINESS

The river-bed is dry.   And dry the flesh
Of the long-dead cat.   Only the drained fur,
In feathers remaining, spreads a lonely fan.

The sober banners lie in stacks, like fallen
                leaves, and
Dry the tight lanterns in the phantom shop:
Empty of the light they wait: they thunder
                under the tread of the spider.
The hot iron of the railroad hisses in the air.

It is early autumn,
Waiting between two festivals; the dumb sky
                thin and blue like egg-shell.
Till the frugal women, the little aunts bent double
With dry aches, shall suck the heated saké
From their brittle claws.

This bareness pleases me, this hard dry air.
The feast will come.   The candle flare
In the paper skull; the skull will grow rosy
And warm; plump fingers ring the cups.
And meanwhile no one talks of national rebirth,
                and no one talks of literary renaissances.